A 28-Day Journal of My Crazy Lesbian Breakup

(And What The Radio Had To Say About It)

Christine Hutman

authorHOUSE®

AuthorHouse™
1663 Liberty Drive, Suite 200
Bloomington, IN 47403
www.authorhouse.com
Phone: 1-800-839-8640

First published by AuthorHouse 6/30/2008

ISBN: 978-1-4343-6237-7 (sc)

Printed in the United States of America
Bloomington, Indiana

This book is printed on acid-free paper.

Disclaimer: Individual's names, as well as the names of certain locations have been changed to protect the identity of those people or entities that may have actually played a part in this debacle.

Contents

Acknowledgements

To my friends, Tara, Amy, Jared, Karen and to my Mom and "Pappa" Don: No matter how many times I fell, you were always there to help me get up and dust me off...I love you all.

To a most beautiful friend, Tiffany Amber: thank you for helping to piece my heart back together.

To Keely Newman, the owner of the Chicago sex toy galleries, Tulip (www.MYTULIP.com): thank you for your encouragement and efforts to help promote this book.

To Kat Fitzgerald (www.MysticImagesPhotography.com): thank you for sharing your gifts of photography, networking and friendship with me.

To my editor, and co-founder of the literary website, www.ThirtyVoices.Wordpress.com, Stacy Jill Jacobs: you came just in time! Know that your contributions were appreciated more than you realize ... (and also know that if any typos are uncovered in this book, I am totally blaming you!) ☺

To my soulmate, Shannon (www.TheShannonGallery.com): Thank you for your love, inspiration, support and all of the work you donated to this project (especially the stunning cover!) I love you, and will "Forever Fall."

And To Shari, My Former Lover:

I believe the world...it did truly spin just for you.

Foreword

It is truly a privilege to say a few words about this wonderful book. Christine's thoughts transitioned to paper are quite amazing. Most entertained, I found I could not put this book down and read it's entirety in virtually one sitting.

As a woman, I could appreciate what Christine went through and my mind entangled my own life experiences with her words. The mixture and balance between comedy and satire helped keep the buoyancy as I anticipated every turned page. I related to the radio references and how they were like bits of a soundtrack to the movie of every breakup I ever endured; I remembered how every favorite song my lovers and I had, seemed to play within that first gut-wrenching hour following the initial realization that the demise of our relationship was imminent.

As a Lesbian, I embraced this story quickly. I believe Christine has linked many fences built around that house which boards a familiar pain, commonly shared by women in love; it is a time that has pulled hard on all of our heartstrings. She has given validation to the fact that we all go through similar relationship derailments, at one time or another; we've all had our share of proverbial "red flags" waving, and perhaps some other foreboding symbols sounding off, and even biting us, along the way. The joys, toys, and non-boy relations, debut and peer out behind the curtain just enough to remind us who we are and what our very special world consists of, as lesbians.

As an artist, I would like to lift my glass to the writer and say, "A job well done," and nod my head in respect. I saw the clarity and character of each friend. I felt the heartfelt challenges, joy, and torment. I appreciated the comical twist.

As Christine's new wife, I had read the book in its entirety, and discovered that even my mixed feelings had mixed feelings. I initially accepted the challenge of reading the story of my True Love's escapades with her ex-girlfriend, and dove in head first, not knowing what to expect, honestly. Surprisingly, I completely fell into "the story" and embraced the most important part - the writing. I truly loved it and believe that a multitude of readers from different backgrounds will too. I also suspect that this is not the last that you will hear of Christine Hutman, and her strong abilities as an artist doing what she does best.

Christine has painted a picture of truth, and not merely a sugar-coated, one-sided view of a victimized martyr's take on a love gone wrong. Leave your rose colored reading glasses on the bed side table . . . This is as real as it gets.

Shannon
May 20, 2008

Introduction

The band Panic! At the Disco makes an excellent point: poise and rationality will be essential in handling this breakup ...

On Monday, March 19th, 2006, at approximately 8pm Central time, I initiated a breakup with my girlfriend of nearly a year over the phone. More accurately, I actually started it but she finished it. Regardless, it was clearly the beginning of the end.

The following diary outlines a stream-of-consciousness account of the next 28 days following our breakup. Why did I think people would be interested in reading this? Let's be honest here: people love drama! What do people love even more than drama? *Other people's* drama! Now add the fact that this drama involves *lesbians*, and you've just moved yourself to the front page of the tabloids!

Admittedly, writing this book involved a certain degree of vulnerability. Outsiders are granted a first hand look at the dysfunction of my relationship, as well as some of my own personal idiosyncrasies. To me, sharing the story of my breakup is the equivalent of being that person sitting in the carnival dunk tank, willing to entertain the masses at my own expense, but for a good cause...

It was my decision to donate 1% of the book's proceeds to benefit one organization in each of the 50 states, which strive to help, support and strengthen our gay and lesbian community.

I believe that something good can come out of something seemingly bad: this is my proof.

It has been said that every experience in life is a learning experience. If this is true, then next time can I just abbreviate this whole estrogen-laden melodrama and opt for the damn correspondence course??

The *Actual* Beginning of the End

This is one of those moments Julian Lennon sang about because it's much "Too Late For Goodbyes".

The air in the car felt so heavy, I almost feared it would suffocate the both of us.

Shari and I were solemnly discussing the evening dinner disaster on the drive home, when halfway back to Shari's, I realized I had forgotten my purse at her mother's house. We had to turn around. (Damn purse! I wasn't even wearing makeup, so what the hell was I carrying at that moment that required bringing a *purse?*)

When we pulled back up in her mother's driveway, we weren't sure who should go inside. It was apparent Shari's mother was angry, so who was better suited to endure a potential confrontation? Shari opted to go in, and looking back on the situation, that was clearly the wrong choice.

Five long minutes passed while I waited in the car and when Shari came out she was in tears. Shari's mother had given her a verbal thrashing about our unenthusiastic presence in her house. In an instant my foulness was resurrected.

We drove home and continued discussing what had transpired during the evening, including her mother's interpretation of our (and particularly my) rude behavior. I admitted that although I was far from engaging, I thought my behavior fell somewhat short of rude, but perhaps I was wrong.

The proverbial icing on the cake came when Shari divulged what her mother had to say regarding an apparently not-too-private conversation I had earlier that evening with Bob, Shari's mother's boyfriend. Shari was able to recite verbatim what Bob and I had discussed (almost) confidentially in the backyard. I was incensed. Shari's mother referenced my statement about "hanging out with the in-laws" and heatedly asked Shari, "IS THAT ALL I AM TO HER??"

I remember responding quite passionately in that instance, and replied with much animation, "Yes Shari, that's ALL she is!" I waited for the gravity of that seemingly loaded question to sink into my lover's consciousness, while I shook my head in disbelief thinking, *"What the hell kind of question was that?"*

We slept at opposite ends of the bed that night.

That was my last trip to Atlanta.

B is for Breakup

Think nobody else understands a broken heart?
Just listen to "Everybody Hurts" by R.E.M

L et's face it. Breakups suck.

When you break up with the love of your life, there may come a time when you reach what feels like the utter depths of despair. You begin to believe that no one can fully appreciate your pain. Your situation was unique. Your relationship was different. Nobody would understand. At this junction, I would encourage you to turn on the radio.

There have been literally *thousands upon thousands* of songs throughout the centuries dealing with love in all of its splendid phases. If you think about it, love is single-handedly responsible for transforming the entire music industry! There are songs that depict every conceivable facet of any relationship including the infatuation of falling in love, the fights, the making up, the great sex, the resurrected fights, the breakup process, the revenge taken against unfaithful lovers, the aftermath of depression, the hopeful reunion, the joy that there was no reunion (or the sorrow that there was), and the sheer bliss of finally finding your lifelong mate. You name it and I guarantee you, *someone* has written a song about it!

Trust me, no matter what your situation is, you are not alone.

It has been my experience that you need a few "false starts" before you really, actually breakup for good. I remember the first time Shari and I attempted to breakup over the phone (Shari was so cute and sounded so serious) but it never stuck because I started laughing! That was my shortest breakup on record. I believe it lasted all of twenty-seven seconds.

The next time we broke up it was about five months into the relationship and it lasted six whole weeks. Many of the problems we had towards the actual end of our relationship could be traced back to a lack of resolution concerning previous stalemates. Unresolved issues *will* come back to haunt you. They do not go away voluntarily; you can not ignore them, or wish them away. Unless you address them properly, they will lie dormant and wait like little piranhas, anxious to gnaw your relationship down to the bone. A friend of mine once told me that the recovery time of a breakup is half the time of the relationship. A stranger once told me that "the best way to get over someone, is to get under someone."

Gee, I think being armed with such an arsenal of helpful and practical information such as that, I'll be just fine in no time!

Day One: Did We Do This ... Really?

*As I say "Bye Bye" to my lover, I'm wishing I had more
of Jo Dee Messina's conviction at the moment...*

With any great breakup comes much confusion, followed by an interesting array of emotions: remorse, denial, anger, and possibly relief (which we may have all experienced on some occasion.) But initially, I think there is a feeling of disbelief, somewhat akin to waking up from a bad dream. You think, "did that really happen, or was I just dreaming?" Then when you catch yourself repeating your habitual pattern of the day, without your partner, it hits you: "Oh, that's right, we're broken up." (Table for one, please.)

My Day One consists of the typical replaying of the conversation from the night before and dissecting the entire breakup. Words are filed away. Phrases are burned into memory. Ammunition is gathered for a future encounter.

It is amazing how memories can affect us physiologically. I mean, to think that just recalling a certain conversation can illicit specific physiological responses as if it were happening *live*, in the moment, is pretty phenomenal if you think about it. If you are like me though, you can even take it a step further and *address* a conversation that isn't happening! So now I am recalling fragments of conversation and interjecting with my own head-shaking and rolling of the eyes, sporadically inserting exclamations such as "incredible" or "unbelievable". (Think of how amusing this might be while sitting in traffic; do not always assume that the person in the car next to you is talking on a hands-free phone.)

I did not waste any time in removing all visible evidence that this relationship had occurred. Pictures, clothing, cards, and all other remnants are immediately put away. It just bothers me too much to see such things out in the open. One thing that amazes me about Shari is her ability (and willingness) to keep photos in their respective places throughout the breakup process; personally, that strikes me as somewhat masochistic, but to each their own.

Earlier today I clipped out a "Love Is" cartoon out of the newspaper. (I know what you're thinking, "What is she, like twelve?") It was sweet and so "us". It was, "Love Is ... wearing his shirt" with the famous little butt-naked blond female wearing an oversized button down shirt. Well, in our case it may not have been *his* shirt, but chances are, it was a *man's* shirt! We liked to wear one another's clothes (which is also an absolute perk of lesbianism, by the way.) I debated back and forth whether I should save it to send to Shari, but I ended up crumpling it up and throwing it away.

I am not fully "upset" at this point because a small part of me still thinks there may be a small possibility that we reconcile…I mean, we have done this before and gotten back together (a few times)…so maybe we just need a few days. Being human, I break one of the unwritten laws in the break up manual and I send a text message. My text message says "I love you and I miss you." Honest and to the point, but some people might consider this cruel and unusual punishment. However, I always operate from the viewpoint of "What if I were hit by a bus today?" What would I have wanted my last words to her to have been? (Did you ever stop to think of what the world would be like if more people not only believed in this philosophy, but actually practiced it?) That is what I felt at the time, so I shared it. Not surprisingly, that text resulted in a phone call that evening.

Relationship experts may not recommend speaking so soon after such a dramatic decision (such as ending a relationship) is made. A "cooling off" period is recommended, but nonetheless, we ventured down this treacherous road. Very soon into the conversation, tears were being shed by my former lover, and we were both left wondering why we thought this conversation was a good idea...

Day Two: Single?

*"Over and over" again, I keep replaying the
entire mess in my head...*

Much like the first day of officially being "broken up", my relationship (or lack thereof) was the first thing on my mind after waking up this morning. It even took precedent over going to the bathroom, for God's sake! Thankfully I didn't have any sad or crazy dreams, so I redirected my thoughts (and headed for the bathroom.)

I think songs and the radio play an interesting part in the breakup process. Note: I did not reference CD's or IPods here. Those are products that require your direction, and if you choose to torture yourself by listening to love songs of your choice that is your business. I want to emphasize the radio's influence here because the power of spontaneity should not be underestimated. Timing is everything, you know. I don't want to appear to be attributing anthropomorphic qualities to the radio, but it is somewhat eerie that it *seems to know* what to play at just the right time. How else would you explain hearing the rarely played "A Real Fine Place to Start" by Sarah Evans, the first love song my ex-girlfriend ever sent to me, on the second day of my breakup? There are no coincidences, you know!

So I am going about my day, marveling at how many times my thoughts are disrupted by thoughts of my ex-girlfriend. I can now believe all of the statistics I hear about how many times men think about sex throughout the day, because I am, without fail, thinking about Shari every ten minutes! Don't misunderstand me: I'm not having sexual thoughts mind you (okay, maybe one or two) but now my thoughts have morphed from breakup-specific memories to the concern of what will happen to all of those *future* plans we made together. What about our commitment ceremony (that we could never agree on where to have?) What about the small pack of dogs we were going to eventually accumulate from the local shelter? There is a contractor somewhere in California that will not make a small fortune off of us by building our custom dream home on the San Diego coastline. (That poor bastard!)

All I can do now is STAY BUSY. Yes. Stay busy and try not to drive those closest to me crazy by enlisting them to help dissect the corpse of my deceased relationship. But what are friends for? Of course they will listen (and listen some more) and side with me (at least initially, anyway.) After some of the emotional bruising has subsided, then I might hear a few hurtful truths. A good friend keeps score for you though (this is particularly true of women) and will remind you of all of those nasty little comments and inconsiderations that your ex was responsible for over the course of your relationship. I personally like to make a list of grievances which I can pull out and review when I am feeling weak; this can be a powerful tool in your recovery. I haven't made that list…yet. I'm still not entirely sure this is our Grand Finale.

We do have the issue of "stuff" though in the form of personal belongings that needs to be exchanged. Well, we didn't live together, so that makes things much easier. It wasn't a nasty breakup where I would have to worry about getting my effects back in little pieces, or collect them off of someone's lawn. Speaking of "stuff", here's a good question: what do you do with the sex toys? (How would you like to see that in a divorce settlement?) I've had this dilemma before. Some of these accessories are too expensive to just throw away, but do you really want to use them with your next partner? What does the rule book say about how much time must elapse between partners with aforementioned toys? See, now there is an advantage to being a biological male: the equipment comes with you. No argument needed!

I sent Shari a very short email: "Please don't trouble yourself sending all of my belongings. I am only interested in X, Y, and Z. The rest you can toss but I would let the Boomer keep the dog bed; he seems to enjoy it and that would be a shame." I was genuinely trying to be considerate, and even though I trust she will send my things, I'm not expecting a reply.

Meet the Players

Shari, what if The Monkees are right? What
if it is "A Little Bit Me, A Little Bit You?"

I was thirty-three years old, living back in my parent's house and teetering on the edge of bankruptcy.

I know you're thinking, "Wow. What a catch." Now before you go making an "L" with your forefinger and thumb and place it on your forehead, allow me to explain…

I took a huge gamble at the age of thirty-two, and started a business in the pet industry. Needless to say, that was a huge gamble I lost. I was in some serious debt. It was a huge blow to me, but I was never completely disheartened. Honestly, in exchange for the experience I had, and the lessons I learned, I am not sorry I tried. This was only a setback in my mind, not a tragedy; I think the tragedy would have been never trying in the first place.

I immediately launched a spin-off business with what resources I had remaining, and began a website called PetServicesReview.com, which was designed to help other entrepreneurs in the pet industry. Shortly after the site's creation, I had the idea to host an upscale networking social for lesbians in the metro Chicagoland area. I went online and joined dating sites to gather opinions and gauge interest in my idea; I made it clear that a relationship was the last thing on my mind!

After speaking with hundreds of lesbians online within a month, I decided just for fun (and out of curiosity) to do a search for someone I might actually want to date (if I were interested in meeting someone, hypothetically.) The results showed that there were a whopping FIVE women scattered across the nation that caught my eye. One of them was my future love interest, Shari, located in Atlanta, Georgia.

I sent her an email comprised of two lines which were very complimentary, and as luck would have it, she responded!

Now for a little coincidental cosmic humor: days before I contacted Shari, she had seen my picture online and read the text I provided. She claimed that she was quite taken with my profile. She assumed that my initial contact to her was in response to me having seen that she read my profile. The only reason she never contacted me was because I lived out of state (and also because I claimed I wasn't seeking anything of a serious nature, just friends.)

We began courting in phases as do the majority of online romancers. We would tell others that ours was a case of "love at first IM". That first day we ended up IMing on the computer for three straight hours. Shari had put a pot of water on the stove to boil pasta when she originally sat down to check her email, and by the end of our conversation she said she was lucky she didn't burn her house down! We were speaking on the phone within three days of our first email, and you couldn't keep us off the phone after that! I was smitten with this woman! After about two weeks of talking extensively to Shari on the phone and exchanging more emails and pictures online, I suggested that we meet halfway. It would have been about a five hour drive for the both of us, but I was completely up for it, and unabashedly excited by the notion. Shari's initial response, however, was not so enthusiastic. She found my idea too spontaneous and a little crazy. (Isn't this the fun part?) I was disappointed and deflated, and didn't go to any length to hide that fact. The thought had even crossed my mind that maybe this wasn't quite a perfect match after all, because I do have tendencies to be…well, spontaneous and a little crazy. After a few days had passed, Shari had warmed up to the idea, and we had finally met (and then it was "love at first sight.")

We managed to see each other on an average every two and half weeks. The upside of the situation was that running a website allowed me the freedom to travel, so I could visit for a week at a time, and sometimes longer.

After about four months of dating, Shari asked me to move to Atlanta to live with her. I felt everything from flattered and elated to scared and skeptical (with a few other miscellaneous emotions in between.) Following much deliberation though, it was determined that I would begin the gradual process of moving and re-establishing my life with my lover in Atlanta.

I was completely forthcoming about my financial situation with Shari from the very beginning. Knowing how close she was with her mother, I requested she share this with her as well (because realistically this is not the kind of information you want to be accidentally stumbled upon later; it could give the appearance of a hidden agenda.) Shari nicknamed me "her little scrapper" because of my passionate persistence and drive. I like to think of myself as being "selectively ignorant" and not being aware of the things I cannot do.

My parents were very supportive of my occupational endeavors. When things took a turn for the worse with my business, they without hesitation committed themselves to helping me any way they could, and for that I am grateful. My entire family comes from a blue-collar background, and although they have never had much monetarily, they are some of the most generous people you would ever meet; I am truly blessed.

My mother and I have a warm and open relationship, but she has never been overly involved in my romantic liaisons. She has no problem with my lifestyle and willingly gives me her input on the women I choose to date. My stepfather is wonderful and has voluntarily taken on the task of rating my girlfriends (particularly aesthetically) and seems to enjoy his job. My biological father has been deceased for a long time. I have no problems with my extended family accepting my lifestyle and I am very open about my orientation to friends, family and work associates.

Shari has a very different set of circumstances. Her entire family shared a conservative, successful, white-collar background. She and her mother are very close. She has a functional, lukewarm relationship with her father; he does not acknowledge Shari's homosexuality and therefore will not support any part of it. She has a brother and sister-in-law who seem to *tolerate* her lifestyle, but would not go out of their way to demonstrate any support. She is not "out" to any work associates or extended family.

Perfect match, wouldn't you say? Gee, when you put it that way, I suppose it was evident we may have had a challenge or two ahead of us! We were dealing with economic differences, distance, the stress of a new business and relationship simultaneously, and semi-closeted homosexuality. Although I think that these compounded issues helped weather away the foundation of our relationship, they didn't amount to the finality of our breakup; they just added fuel to another, bigger fire...

Too Close for Comfort

Jack Johnson gave me a heads up in his song, "Flake": the relationship might not work out because of other ties...

"Come sit next to me...*right here*" Shari's mother said as she patted the vinyl of the restaurant booth seat.

There were four of us to be seated at a half-round corner booth in the restaurant: me, Shari, Shari's mother and the mother's best friend, Lilly; Shari's mother was trying to orchestrate the seating arrangement so that she could sit next to me, and became somewhat frustrated when this did not occur. Shari interjected and convinced her mother that it would be more conducive for conversation to be sitting *across* from me during our first meeting, rather than next to me.

"So, tell us a little about yourself" came the request from Shari's mother.

I felt a little uncomfortable with the concentrated focus and declined to say too much, adhering to modesty. The woman, clearly on a mission and not to be thwarted, responded by asking, "Well, then, what would you like to know about *me*?" I remember thinking, "This is interesting." I had a *Dream On* moment just then, as a scene from the movie *Beaches* popped into my head: Bette Midler said "That's enough about me. What about you? What do you think about me?"

We had managed to have an overall cordial first dinner together, despite the occasional awkward moments, and I remember having had a very nice time with the family friend, Lilly. She was a naturally jovial woman who was very lively and we hit it off well instantly. As we were all leaving the restaurant, Shari's mother said to Lilly with intentional volume, "I think you'd be better off being Shari's mom. Christine obviously likes you better" as she pretended to pout. I questioned Shari about this occurrence on the ride home. Shari said she felt something was "off" between the two of us, but didn't find anything extraordinarily peculiar about her mother's behavior. I thought to myself, "nothing peculiar?" It appeared that "interesting" was about to get much more interesting.

In the very beginning of my relationship with Shari, before her mother and I had ever met, we began laying the groundwork for something unique. On a few occasions Shari's mother had been inspired to call me on my cell phone. She would be out with Shari, and if I were to come up in conversation, her mother would just spontaneously suggest, "Let's call Christine!"

"What?!" my friends would exclaim upon hearing this. "What the hell is she calling you for?"

"I don't know" I responded at the time. To the best of my recollection, none of my other lovers' mothers had ever called me wanting to chit-chat, but I gathered it was some way of initiating some kind of "girlfriendly" status with me. She was obviously trying to bond with me on some level, which at the time I wrote off as merely a sweet gesture. My girlfriend shared with me that her mother had made a few comments about pictures she had seen of me which could be described as quite complimentary, to say the least. The one comment that did take us both slightly aback was her reference to my cleavage, but we managed to share a laugh about it.

While I was in town Shari's mother offered to take me out to lunch for the sake of "getting me out of the house" while my girlfriend was at work, and I was working from her home. Shari's mother had stated that she wanted a chance to get to know me in a "less distracting setting" where it could be just the two of us. I appreciated the offer to break the monotony of my routine during the afternoon, so I accepted. Lunch was pleasant enough, and conversation was light but when it was over, I couldn't help but feel as though the woman was clearly disappointed that it wasn't more fulfilling in some way. I was correct because she had even voiced her dismay to her daughter.

As months passed, Shari's mother and I would encounter one another when I would be in town; it was a ritual for mother and daughter to go to dinner together once a week, so if I happened to be in town, then I was expected to partake in the festivities. Some dinners went better then others. The main complaints against me, which became a regular occurrence, were that I generally didn't demonstrate enough interest in Shari's mother and that I demonstrated *too much* interest in the jovial family friend, Lilly, when she would accompany us. From that moment forward, there were specific instances when the family friend was purposefully excluded from dinner to alleviate this situation.

Then things had taken a more confrontational turn one evening…

Shari and I met Shari's mom and Lilly for dinner, and after briefly discussing the seating arrangement yet again, began partaking in some casual dinner conversation. Quite abruptly, without warning, Shari's mother addressed me very clearly and said, "You and I are going to get along." I laughed it off and continued the previous stream of friendly conversation. By now, my thesis regarding mom's unorthodox behavior had come together; I felt I had a full grasp of what was occurring here. I gathered from the first dinner that mom needs *a lot* of attention. I could appreciate this, to a degree; I had been known to have a high-maintenance moment myself from time to time. I had gathered from this dinner tonight that Shari's mother was telling me in no uncertain terms that I *would not* be interfering in their special mother-daughter relationship. My interpretation was that perhaps she felt mildly threatened as if I were going to somehow take her daughter away from her, or disrupt their relationship. Believe me, the *last* thing I wanted to do was interfere here! I had even discussed my observations with Shari, and went so far as to volunteer to stay back at the house on various occasions, so as to *not* interrupt their regularly scheduled dinner plans; that option didn't sit well with Shari though. (Damned if I do; damned if I don't.)

I was a bit confused by her mother drawing proverbial lines in the sand but displaying a determination to ingrain herself in my life: was this an example of keeping your friends close and your enemies closer? What was this woman's M.O.?

A little time had passed and again Shari's mother addressed me, this time by adding, "You and I *are going* to get along, because I'M HERE TO STAY. I'm not going anywhere."

At this junction, I felt as though perhaps Shari should intervene. I could guarantee that had the roles been reversed, no family member of mine would have *ever* confronted Shari in this manner while I sat idly by; it was not only utterly inappropriate, but I personally would have died of embarrassment! I kicked Shari under the table to cue her to consider reeling her mother in; *Shari never responded* because apparently she was too engrossed in sheepishly counting the floor tiles. Now I had lost my patience with this display at the dinner table, and the fact that my girlfriend didn't want to "get in the middle" of the situation. Was this really the time or place to be having this discussion? I fear my signature bluntness had gotten the best of me at that moment, and I pointedly asked Shari's mother the previously suppressed questions that only a potently concocted (and happily consumed) Margarita could inspire: "WHAT IS IT THAT YOU WANT FROM ME?? Are you looking to have some moonlit-running-through-the-woods-naked-while-holding-hands-womyn's-bonding ritual with me?!" At that point, Lilly interjected by inserting a humorous story about herself going to a beach and losing her bikini top in the ocean (speaking of nakedness.) Shari and I would end up discussing that evening on several occasions in the future.

Believe it or not, we managed to have a few pleasant dinners after that incident. I even took it upon myself to invite Shari's mother and the mother's boyfriend, Bob, over to Shari's house for a steak dinner one evening, taking special care of all of the arrangements myself. Things went very well, and she seemed to appreciate the gesture. At the end of the evening we would have one of our signature lingering hugs (you know the kind where *you* stop hugging, but the other person hasn't released you, so you find yourself continuing to hug them in somewhat of a trapped state) and we appeared to finally be getting along…or so I thought.

During my last visit to Atlanta, Shari and I went out to dinner with Lilly, Shari's mother and Bob. Shari's mother provided us the entertaining topic of possibly "switching teams" as she considered dating women herself; although this conversation was *clearly* in jest, it was not the first we had heard of it. She had even gone so far to brag about a potential "girlfriend" she had, in the form of a lesbian massage therapist who worked at her country club. We played along with the theme of the evening, but did impress upon the woman that her headaches with dating men would not necessarily be alleviated by dating women; it would just bring new and different headaches.

In the past, certain inquiries made by Shari's mother would bother her daughter. "I hate when my mother asks me what we are going to do while you're in town. And I *absolutely* used to hate when she would ask me what we would do when we would drive to meet halfway in Nowheresville! What on earth does she *think* we are going to do?"

I would agree that it wasn't appropriate to make such inquiries. The woman knows damn well that if we haven't seen each other in two weeks, we are meeting (in essence) in the middle of a prairie, and we have a hotel room for the weekend, then chances are good that that hotel room is going to put to good use! (Insert your own adult interpretation here.)

So at this particular dinner when Shari's mother leaned forward across the table from me and suggestively asked me what we were going to do during the rest of my visit, I thought I would cut her off at the pass. I leaned forward, smiling deviously and replied, "I can't tell you about the things that we are going to be doing", honestly thinking that my risqué response may have killed the curious cat. Imagine my surprise when she looked me right in the eyes, smiled back and responded, "I *like* the things that you think you can't tell me about." I turned slowly to look at Shari as I raised one eyebrow and smiled.

General conversation continued and Shari's mother proposed that before I left Atlanta, Shari and I should come over to her house the following week so that she could cook dinner for us. "I *insist*! Anything you like" Shari's mother offered. Dinner was then planned for the following week, and although I was grateful for the invitation, a small part of me couldn't help but think that with tonight's dinner going as well as it had, perhaps we would have been better off leaving well enough alone; I wasn't anxious to press my luck.

When it was time to leave the restaurant, we all began exchanging our goodbyes for the evening, and as I received my usual warm, lengthy embrace from Shari's mother she said, "I love you." I was so caught off guard in that instant, that all I could manage awkwardly in return was, "Oh….That's so sweet…Thank you."

Driving on the way home, I said to Shari, "Well, your mother told me she loves me."

"What?! Oh boy! She said that?" Her surprise was apparent.

"Yes she did. And all this time we weren't sure if she even *liked* me!"

Following Shari's "Hmph", it was fairly quiet for the duration of the ride home.

The day came the following week when we were supposed to go to Shari's mother's house for dinner, but there was one small problem: I did NOT want to go. I absolutely, undeniably, and admittedly did NOT want to go to dinner that evening. The feeling had started early that morning, but as the day wore on it had festered into almost a full-blown, inexplicable feeling of *dread*. A few hours before we were to arrive, I told Shari over the phone (for she was still at work) of my ill-feelings; she informed me that it was too late to cancel. Maybe she could tell her mother I developed a migraine, and she could go without me? That solution was inadequate; I was going to dinner.

I called my friend Amy, back in Chicago, on the way to Shari's work where we were meeting to ride together to Shari's mother's house. I begged Amy to give me a pep talk to help motivate me for this impending dinner. I could not for the life of me muster the energy to put on a performance for Shari's mother that evening, and was growing resentful that that was exactly what was being expected of me. Amy suggested I stay home, but when I told her that wasn't an option, she told me to focus on the fact that it would be a quick dinner, and her word of advice was not to talk too much that evening. I actually began saying positive affirmations aloud in the car in an attempt to turn the tide.

Unfortunately, by the time I reached Shari I could hardly hide my lack of enthusiasm about having to go to dinner; I didn't even bother to put on any makeup for the occasion (which did not go unnoticed.) My dull mood immediately impacted Shari when we met up, and her mood began to become rather sedate in response.

Shari's mother immediately detected something was amiss when we arrived. I was rather apathetic and unusually quiet, Shari was acting strangely because of my mood, and Shari's mother was completely thrown off by the situation. After arriving we learned that Bob would be joining us for dinner, and he was running a little late; this only added to my growing foulness because now a quick dinner was becoming a prolonged event.

Eventually when Bob arrived things did get better, gradually. He and I went outside and chatted while he cooked the steaks. Sensing something was out of the norm, he asked me what was wrong. I explained to him that it had just been a very long day, and that I was a little irritated with work concerns because my website had been experiencing a few recent technological glitches. "This just wasn't the ideal day to hang out with the in-laws" I confessed between the two of us. He empathized, and shared a few work stories of his own, which helped lighten the mood further.

Although by the end of dinner, I felt considerably better and Shari's mood had improved, we received an icy parting from Shari's mother on the way out.

My family and friends were becoming mildly disturbed by what I was describing to them as the relationship between Shari's mother and I unfolded. During a conversation with my own mother about the matter, she surprised me with her bluntness by asking, "Do you think she has the hots for you?"

"I don't know. I'm trying not to read too much into this stuff. Maybe I'm wrong. Maybe I'm overreacting." Then I asked my mother "As a mom, could you see doing or saying some of those things to any one of *my* exes? How about Tara? Tara's always been your favorite." She gave me a half puzzled, half disgusted look as though she had just eaten a bad piece of proscuttio.

I guess I had my answer.

There is always the possibility I could be 500% wrong about the entire situation. Things always look worse when you take them out of context, right? After all, I have been known to have a very healthy ego and an active imagination to match. I needed to consult rational, objective council. I needed to ensure that I was taking all possible perspectives into consideration.

When I was back in Chicago, I called upon the expertise of my sister, Lisa. My sister, who is five years older than me, is one of the greatest problem solvers I have ever met (so long as it's someone else's problem.) This is not to say that my sister is without some eccentricities of her own, such as the inablitity and (and utter unwillingness) to eat soft serve ice cream in a cup if some of villain has tainted the perfect swirl by flattening it with a lid. (A fascinating psychosis, I think.) We decided to meet at the coffeehouse, The Fat Bean, in Naperville for conversation and chocolate (both clearly being of equal importance.) The Fat Bean is a rare treasure, being as it is one of the only gay-friendly coffeehouses in Chicago's Western suburbs. The café was well-equipped with a delectable variety of coffees and desserts capable of momentarily soothing the most drama-laden lesbian heartache. My plan was to convince my sister that all of my concerns were unwarranted, that there was nothing inappropriate occurring between Shari's mother and me, and then my sister would in turn, hopefully convince me that what I had just told her was reality. Unfortunately, my sister was not an easy sell, and furthermore took advantage of the opportunity to articulate that if anyone is well-versed in the art of flirting, it is me, so *I* should know! (She may very well have a point there.)

I decided to approach this from a different direction: I asked my sister if I was wrong for feeling (for lack of a better word) "patronized" by sharing my concerns with my girlfriend who was completely disinterested in my distress. My main complaint was that I frequently felt as though I was putting in more effort and energy to appease my lover's *mother* than I was my own *lover*! It was a continual stream of "Look at me, sit next to me, talk to me, don't talk to her, look at me more, laugh at my jokes, sit closer…" I COULDN'T TAKE IT ANYMORE!!!

My sister empathized with my frustration and stated that an intimate relationship is ideally designed to be between *two* people.

At one point I had joked with Lisa and said that if such a future situation ever presented itself again, and a perceived flirtation occurred, I should just grab Shari's mother and plant one of the hottest kisses I could muster right on her lips! In my mind it was a win-win situation: either I would be completely wrong about my assessment and therefore the woman would be traumatized to the point of (hopefully) leaving me alone or I would be completely right and then my girlfriend could see that my powers of perception really weren't all that faulty. My sister didn't think the idea was a good one, in light of the latter possibility; she was afraid that I might start something that I wasn't prepared to finish.

It reminded me of something a former business associate told me once about the lurking lustiness of senior citizens: "Just because there's snow on the mountain, doesn't mean there's not fire in the hole."

On second thought, I think for future reference I will heed my sister's advice.

Day Three: Torture, anyone?

*The band Goldfinger hit it right on the head because
I find that I'm "Still Counting the Days"…*

I always check my email first thing in the morning. I admit it, I'm addicted. The ex and I had a ritual of exchanging morning emails, and I haven't gotten quite used to the fact that they aren't coming anymore. Suddenly my e-mailbox is quite empty…and lonely. Now I think I know where all of those so-called "spiders" that crawl statistically all over the internet gather for a little R and R…in the cozy confines of my desolate e-mail box! I did get something in the form of an email that amused me, though. The subject line read: YOU HAVE SEVEN DAYS TO FIND YOUR SOULMATE. Oh my! How ominous! Am I to be hit by a bus after all? When I opened it, it was a free 7-day trial to an online personals site for dog lovers! (Am I not the butt of some cosmic joke?)

As the day wore on, Shari and I decided to embark upon a playful exchange of text messages throughout the day, consciously ignoring the "no contact" rule mentioned previously. My friends and family were placing bets on how long our breakup will actually last. (We have done this before, obviously.) Today was Shari's day off, and she was spending it with her mother. (Later I inquired somewhat sarcastically, but genuinely curious if this involved celebration and many margaritas.)

By evening we were speaking on the telephone, rehashing the entire series of events which has led to Monday night's decision. We were very thorough, but evidently getting nowhere.

I was getting very frustrated and considered speaking in another language to make some more headway. We couldn't even agree on why we broke up in the first place! Not to say that this is a mandatory requirement, by any means, but there is a peace of mind in having some final agreement. I don't like to think that we are (or were) so out of sync that we can't see the situation for what it really is…what would that say about the rest of the relationship? Were we using two different operating manuals the whole time?

At this point, it was becoming increasing evident that Shari was under the direct influence of her mother. She was actually starting to *sound* like her, frighteningly enough! An interesting revelation she did share was that earlier that day her mother remarked (to both of our surprise) that Shari and I "worked well together" and we "just had problems where outsiders were concerned." YOU DON'T SAY??? I believe my ex is too close to the situation to see things objectively, and will even venture to make the same claim for myself to be fair (but I do believe I am a *little* more objective.)

I threw out one last ditch effort (which I have in the past, knowing that it would be rejected) and that is the dreaded "T" word: therapy. We needed an unbiased mediator to give us feedback on this situation. The initial response was a sarcastic one: "well, seeing as we are no longer a couple, I guess we don't need couple's counseling." I pointed out the inappropriateness of that jab, to which she promptly apologized. In the past I had heard excuses of why we should not go which included the lack of practicality because of our distance, and the ever-famous: if we needed counseling this soon in our relationship then we were clearly doomed. I have been to counselors independently and in other relationships in the past, and most counselors seem to agree that it is a *good* thing to see a counselor earlier on in a relationship to help squash small issues as they arise, which will deter large, seething resentments later. (All in favor?)

Her response to this was: if she really, really felt deep down that it would impact the situation, she would go, but she is not convinced.

I was so angry I could start speaking in tongues! That's it! I was done! I have wasted enough time this evening and will not go on one minute more!

We ended the conversation abruptly. This is madness! What was I thinking???

Day Four: Odds and Ends

I like Avril Lavene's attitude right about now: screw her, screw her friends and screw the fantasy of "My Happy Ending"...

Today I am gathering up Shari's belongings and preparing to send them back to her. At times like these, as you are exorcising the ghosts of your former lover from your surroundings, you will inevitably keep stumbling upon remnants of your relationship in tucked away places. For example, I had forgotten about the computer file folder labeled "Baby" which contained photos from happier times. I did not forget about the special computer file folder however which contains several steamy emails that I would pray no one would ever accidentally stumble upon (although Penthouse might pay a good penny for them!)

I made my list today: the infamous list. It is a list of grievances and shortcomings about my partner that is to be referred to in moments of extreme weakness and/ or emotional upheaval. Some points are undesirable characteristics while others were specific instances which may have spelled out a disturbing pattern. After reading something like that, in reflection, you wonder "what the hell was I thinking, dating that person?" And that is *exactly* what it is designed to do! As the day progressed, I added more little notes here and there. We've all heard the saying "opposites attract", but I think I may want to challenge this theory. It seems like even though we had several things in common, we had some serious fundamental differences. One of the biggest pet peeves I had marked on my list is that her spaces have a propensity to get cluttered. I don't do clutter at all! It's so anti-feng shui. I will say though in her defense, that as I brought these things to her attention, they were eventually rectified (albeit somewhat reluctantly.)

It's entertaining to read the list to another friend (preferably one who has been privy to the entire drama as it has unfolded.) Their own interjections can make for fun additives. However, the act of sharing your lover's shortcomings or blunt faults with friends can also be a double-edged sword, though. Many times your friends will regurgitate this information at unsolicited times, so you must be very careful with this dispensing of information. Case in point: one of my ex's friends, being the good friend that she is, is still keeping score from our *last* breakup. Sadly enough, I never fell into good favor with that particular friend again. Shari has a theory about this though: her friend is bent out of shape seven ways because *her* ex (that she is still pining for) doesn't want *her* back, so why on earth would she be cheering *us* on? Misery loves company, you know! Ah, the complexities of being a woman!

Shari and I shared an email and a text today. She claims she is "not handling this well." She wants me to know she loves me and misses me.

Perhaps she should make a list of her own.

The Joys of Lesbianism

"I Kissed A Girl" and I'm definitely doing it again!

Despite what you may have read, heard or seen, I am here to dispel a few myths concerning the often sensationalized, mostly misrepresented world of lesbianism. As much as the pop culture would like to encourage every man's fantasy by painting a picture of two supermodels running around together, playfully holding hands, flaunting their sexuality for drooling onlookers everywhere, and label them "lesbians", this is simply not the case. Oh, I agree this behavior happens regularly in any-happening-downtown-dance-club every weekend, but these are not *lesbians*. These are straight women (or bisexual women at best) exploiting the situation to get a little bonus attention. (The irony here is that I am tempted to encourage this behavior because at least from a purely superficial viewpoint these women really would make some good representatives!)

The reality of the situation is that lesbianism is much less glamorous aesthetically and emotionally than most people realize (and this is working under the assumption that adequate thought has been given to the topic of the lesbian lifestyle at all.) I suppose it is somewhat presumptuous of me to think that we lesbians, as a subdivision of the gay community, have become a kind of Eighth Wonder of the World.

Without offending the entire lesbian community in one single-handed swoop, akin to some international slap in the face, suffice it to say when describing the physicality of most (I didn't say all) lesbians or lesbian couples, they do NOT look like the couple of women on the cover of your Vivid Video box of porn sitting in your closet. Not even close! Sorry!

From an emotional standpoint, two women together can experience levels of intimacy that are exquisitely indescribable, which stands to reason, seeing as women are emotionally-driven creatures, unlike our logically-driven male counterparts. Cuddling marathons, holding hands, washing one another's hair, talking, and partaking in a variety of other soft and luxurious exchanges would make most men shudder. (I'm not even sure if the word "cuddle" is in the male vocabulary.) Women are generally soft, sweet, gentle, and nurturing beings. Women like to "nest" and become instantaneously domestic with one another; the relationship is comfortable and feels natural. Why do you think the joke "What does a lesbian bring on a second date? A U-Haul" is so popular?

What is the flip side of all of this emotional intimacy, you wonder? (Ever heard the saying that you can have too much of a good thing?) I have always believed that women are certainly the more dangerous of the two sexes *because* we are emotionally driven. We don't just know logically how to hurt our partner, but we know almost instinctively where to inflict the most pain possible with more expediency and precision than a heat-seeking missile. We can be manipulative, vicious, bitchy, jealous and possessive. "Hell hath no fury … " so the saying goes!

Picture if you will a hypothetical scenario of a man and a woman in a romantic involvement where an (alleged, but grave) injustice has occurred. Maybe the man has been accused of flirting, or worse, of being unfaithful. Our female's emotions are running high, instincts are flaring, imaginations are working overtime, tears are welling … Let's assume the man is 100% innocent. You may feel some empathy, knowing the lengths he will have to go to in an attempt to rectify the situation: he reassures her (or attempts to), explains, apologizes, explains some more, and after all is said and done, his efforts prove futile; he still ends up sleeping on the couch.

Let's add some complexity to the situation: two women are in the same scenario. Let's assume that the woman being accused is 100% innocent as well. You might want to reserve your empathy for an unsuspecting bystander, should this individual be unfortunate enough to be witness to this potential catfight. A psycho-emotional game of chess ensues, and it might play out something like this: it begins when one woman launches an accusation towards the other about being unfaithful. The woman accused is deeply hurt by the accusation, and lashes back angrily because how could her lover *dare* question her love and loyalty?? The suspicious lover reads into this defensive reaction an obvious display of guilt and drives forward the attack. Being pushed once more, the accused woman may interpret this as a kind of reverse-psychology and thinks that maybe *her lover* is actually guilty of some infidelity, because where else could this all be coming from?? Now the accused woman may bring to the surface something that she has stifled for quite awhile. She has been storing little nuggets of suspicions, and hording them away like a calculating little squirrel. The accused woman abruptly confesses that she was never comfortable with how friendly that male mechanic down the street was with her lover when they brought the car in for oil changes. In a perverse twist of imagination fueled by passion she convinces herself that her lover even seemed to *enjoy* the flirtation (despite her lover's adamant claims that she is *not* bisexual.) Yes, it all makes sense now! This is what it is really all about: it has to do with that mechanic down the street! THAT SLUT!

Now, to add fuel to the fire, let me offer a little hormonal sabotage: what if one of the women is PMSing? (Everyone enjoys a good fireworks display, right?) What about the WORST case scenario: what if BOTH women are PMSing?? (I am suddenly envisioning Robot from *Lost in Space* waving his arms frantically screaming "DANGER! DANGER, WILL ROBINSON!")

Yes, I believe it is a fair assessment to compare the passion of a lesbian relationship to the proverbial double-edged sword ... which reminds me, if you ever do find yourself in the aforementioned scenario as witness or participant, be sure to rid the immediate area of all sharp, cutting instruments.

Things could get messy rather quickly.

Day Five: The Power of the Subconscious

It's just me and Staind, "Right Here" …and waiting.

I used to have dreams when my girlfriend and I were still together about dating other women. (That's never a good sign.) Although the dreams were never explicit, this was mildly troublesome, nonetheless. (If that level of discomfort is not adequate for your personal taste, then by all means, make the mistake of sharing those dreams with your lover! You will have fodder for months and possibly years to come!)

Yesterday, I was speaking to Tara, another ex-girlfriend of mine from several years past. We have a wonderful, friendly relationship. She had some exciting news to share, and an interesting game ensues over the telephone:

"Guess who's gay!" she says.

(Ah, the old "guess who's gay" game!)

"I don't know. Who?" comes my answer.

"Suze Orman!" she states delightedly.

"We already knew that!" I respond disappointedly.

"I know, but it's always exciting to hear it confirmed."

I must agree.

Several years ago, Tara and I met Suze Orman at a financial seminar in Chicago. Her orientation was pretty apparent to us then; she registered on the "gaydar". We all had our picture taken together and I remember she affectionately called us her "lovebugs." I always did find her attractive, despite a substantial age difference. So, now I will take this whole conversation between the two of us and file it away into my subconscious.

It released itself last night in the form of a semi-erotic dream about being in a swimming pool one evening with Suze Orman! Oh my!

I text message my friend, Amy, this morning with the news of my nocturnal adventure. The reply comes, "You have a vivid imagination." That's an understatement!

In the early afternoon, I received a quite unexpected text from Shari. She acknowledged my email from yesterday, and asked if I was going to attend any pet trade shows this weekend. I playfully responded with an accusation that she is attempting to make small talk under the guise of work inquiries. One more brief text follows in response.

I'm still not feeling the full effect of this breakup, actually. Conversations we have had in the past regarding our last, 6-week breakup led to the revelation that she was "miserable" during that time. I have been miserable in the past during other breakups, and thank every God I can think of that I do not feel that way presently. I do not want to feel that way, and I would never, EVER wish those feelings on anyone! I've had my share of letter-writing-while-sobbing, depression-dwelling episodes when I was much younger, and I never want to revisit that seventh layer of Hell again! I am convinced that in the midst of a particularly difficult breakup, you really *do* temporarily lose your mind! There is absolutely no talking logically to anyone in that state; there is nothing that you can do or say for the heartbroken, they just have to come out the other side on their own. Personally, I have found a more "gradual" breakup works best for me, with the primary goal being: friendship. As you can see, I do not like to "cut and run" but gently back out of a situation; much less tumultuousness in my opinion. I think one of the saddest things I have ever heard of is when couples have been together for ten or twenty-plus years, they separate, *but never speak again*! Or they *hate* one another. I cannot wrap my mind around this concept. You spent a percentage of your lifetime loving this other person, your partner, and then nothing? Not even civility? Obviously, I do not have a problem remaining in contact with exes, and I would not give my partner a problem either, although admittedly in my younger years, I wasn't quite so secure.

I ended up calling Shari after her work day for friendly chit-chat. The conversation remained lighthearted, and we shared everyone else's observations about our alleged breakup with one another. We ended the conversation nicely, and joked that we would probably speak tomorrow. She had yard work to tend to, and I had to get ready to have dinner with my sister, Lisa. Apparently this was quite the exciting Saturday night for everyone.

After reflecting on the entire exchange shortly thereafter, I sent her a text asking if we could speak tonight, after I returned from dinner. She stated that she would like that. I realize the craziness in speaking every day and want to put that out there- we really need to start to cut the connection (or could this still be salvaged?) I know, I know! Most of the connecting is on my part, and I take responsibility for that! So I will politely excuse myself in the very near future. It is just a cycle of masochistic behavior, and it must stop. I am doing my "backing out" behavior; I just need to back my ass up a little faster (and out the door!) I hate, hate, hate to admit it, but I am actually entertaining the thought of (dare I say it) *making up with her mother* but I'm not sure exactly what that would entail…

Lisa met me at the family's house and we drove downtown together. My sister was having no more luck finding a stable, heterosexual relationship, and on some level perhaps I could have found solace in this, knowing that good relationships are difficult to find regardless of your orientation, but I did not.

On the car ride downtown we started to compare notes, and unofficially try to "one-up" the other about whose situation is worse. We make threats to switch to each other's side, the "other side" (because we all know the grass is greener there.) We complain, analyze, and wonder, all while laughingly continuing our mobile-therapy road show heading into the city.

My sister came up with a possible alternative solution to her own problem: become a professional escort. Her rationale isn't all that faulty.

She wants material things. Men want sex. Instead of suffering through the mechanics and falsehood of trying (yet again) to make a relationship work, why not drop the act and just call it what it is. Although I don't encourage this new found philosophy of hers, I can certainly appreciate her argument.

We discuss the marvels of the many forms of modern communication we have at our disposal these days. We have instant gratification via various technological outlets: email, cell phones and text messaging. Lisa makes me laugh with her re-enactment of the frustration she has felt when she does not receive her expected dose of instant gratification because the person she is trying to contact is not responding quite instantly enough. That is the whole point, isn't it? This leads to my sister questioning the technological aptitude of her phone, and the quality of her entire phone service in general. Is the phone working properly? Does she have a signal? Did the call actually go through? I found all of this very amusing because at times I can be much the same way.

Once we reached our destination, our mutual counseling session was paused only long enough to order various tapas dishes complete with Sangria and Margaritas, which was just what the doctor would have ordered (would he not have had his medical license revoked.)

We shared laughs, frustrations, predictions and even show one another stored text messages in our phones. This led to the both of us actually sending texts to the objects of our affection, while still in the restaurant, in between courses. How pathetic! Here I was, in downtown Chicago on a Saturday night in a festive restaurant, in an attempt to have a good time and forget about Shari (at least temporarily) and here I was texting her! Nice. My sister, strongly encourages me (the non-drinker that I am) to have a second margarita. We are going to have a good time, even if it is at the expense of my liver, damn it! I sent a text to Shari notifying her of this. Shari playfully responds, "I don't know who this is, but what have you done with Christine." My sister never did get any response to her text.

I have observed over the years, and have heard this said by many men, that when women complain about a certain problem, they do not necessarily want a resolution. They just complain for the sake of complaining…I have seen this in action, myself, but my sister and I both seem to favor resolution. The act of speaking out loud, of sharing thoughts, can offer priceless enlightenment oftentimes. In this case though, my sister and I both know what we need to do, it is just a matter of doing it.

We left the restaurant and began our four block walk back to the car which we had parked on the street. We were by no means drunk, not even tipsy, but my sister held me around the waist as we window shopped our way back to the car. Perhaps it was the act of two women walking in such an intimate fashion, maybe it was the effects of Saturday night, or possibly a full moon, but men were driving by and honking and whistling (such obnoxious creatures they can be at times.)

We walked up the street. No car. We walked down the street. Still no car. This is ridiculous! Are we actually intoxicated, just not paying attention, or is my stigmatism stronger than I give it credit for?

We crossed the street in an attempt to look for the car from a different angle. As we began our search anew for what felt like the hundredth time, we passed the open doorway of a lively gay bar as a small group of vivacious, attractive female impersonators were leaving. My sister and I had inadvertently merged into the group of three performers who quite boisterously explained that they were celebrating one of the entertainer's birthdays, who happened to be a very pretty Latina with incredibly sculpted eyebrows. (I admit it: I was jealous.) They shared that they were now on their way to work at another bar. I said that I was a bit surprised that they were celebrating before work, but they assured me that the party would certainly continue later as well.

The previous spectacle of my sister and I was nothing compared to the sight of the two of us engulfed by this celebratory (and somewhat intoxicated) troupe moving merrily down the street. Admittedly, we were somewhat distracted by all of the encompassing activity, and therefore were not looking for the car as meticulously as we should have been at this point.

Our revelry was cut short by the appearance of a shoddy, late model, white Cutlass driving by with four Hispanic men inside. The car slowly passed us from the opposite direction we were heading, and with both windows rolled down, the occupants inside began yelling at our group. The insults hurled from the car were in Spanish, and although I am not a fluent speaker of the romance languages, I easily deducted that they were in fact specific insults directed towards the performers.

Our birthday girl immediately set off a counter attack, spewing foreign obscenities at a velocity that would have made Charo jealous. The only word that I recognized from a college Spanish class was "zapato", and at precisely the moment the word registered in my dusty memory, our Latin beauty had taken off one of her high heels, and brandished it fiercely overhead! Fueled by a South American passion (and a previous consumption of some expensive tequila) she took off to charge the car! Shrieks emitted from her two companions, horror seized my sister and I, and instinctively we all ran after the feisty Latina, who luckily hadn't gotten too far ahead of us! We all grabbed on to whatever piece of her was available, and I had ended up getting a handful of sequenced dress in the small of her back; had I been alone though, I imagine it would have been much like trying to reign in a wild Clysdale single-handedly! The car full of offenders sped off quite content with their havoc, and we spent the next few minutes trying to calm down the feisty birthday girl.

We resumed our walk down the street, and after Lisa and I calculated that we had reached the furthest boundary outlining where we could have possibly parked the car, we had to bid our new friends a good evening. Hugs and cheek kisses were exchanged, and my sister and I parted with free passes to an upcoming performance and a few phenomenal make up tips.

We hailed a cab and had him drive us back up the street, embarrassed by our situation, and finally found the car. As we headed home, we recapped the craziness of the evening's events.

When I finally got in it was later than I anticipated. I was sure Shari was asleep but she wanted to be notified of my safe arrival home. I should have sent her a text message, but made the mistake of calling. She was drowsy and admittedly crabby because she had been doing her best to fend off sleep while waiting for my call. She didn't want to talk, and recommended continuing this tomorrow. I was left feeling somewhat deflated.

What a surprise.

Through Good Times...

"Hey There Delilah", know that if someone is willing to travel a thousand miles to see you, you must be pretty special ...

"You put the life in my life."

That was the last significant expression of love that I received from Shari prior to our breakup, and I remember being particularly touched by her sentiment; ironically, that was just days before everything started to fall apart. I knew exactly what she meant though as she was explaining to me how desolate things would become when my dogs and I would leave her to come back to Chicago for a few weeks. Your life is completely transformed when you are in love: the days are happier, colors are brighter, food tastes better (you get the idea.)

Baby Girl, Baby Lover, Lover Baby, My Love, and My Soulmate.

We had some really good times.

Whether we were watching reruns of *Absolutely Fabulous* or *The Family Guy* cuddled together in her overstuffed lounge chair in the living room, reading together outside in the sunshine sipping homemade lemonade, preparing fondue for dinner on a Saturday night or a fabulous brunch for Sunday morning, with her is right where I wanted to be. Shari was loving, affectionate, intelligent, ambitious, attractive and more.

We were perfect together.

We had things in common: she could ride a unicycle and juggle. I had mastered the stilts and could juggle. We would joke that if we started a family we could double as a circus troupe.

We learned from one another: she taught me how to dance the two-step (which to Shari's amusement I commonly referred to as "being pushed around backwards in circles") and I taught her how to dance the meringue. She taught me to have an appreciation for color catchers in the laundry's wash cycle, and I taught her the value of keeping a Dustbuster in the bathroom and baby wipes in the car.

I was a diplomatic, romantic Libra and she was a devoted, attentive Gemini; the astrology books said we were a good match.

I told her that she was the closest thing to perfection I had ever found in a partner, and I meant it; she had so many qualities I sought in a mate.

I have a collection of sweet memories interspersed with some humorous ones. One particular memory which struck me as both sweet and humorous occurred on a day we were preparing to walk the dogs on the forest trails near Shari's home. It was a bit chilly outside, and the weather necessitated a hat and gloves. Shari chose to wear a beige coat, but donned a yellow hat, red scarf and green gloves. I remember saying, "Honey, you look like a traffic light!" She laughed, although mildly embarrassed. We then walked the dogs through the winding trails, holding hands and sneaking kisses amid occasional joggers until some erratic canine behavior would force us to pay more attention to the matter at hand.

Another humorous memory that at least had sweetness potential was the day I was ridding the house of dead plants. For whatever reason Shari had accumulated quite a collection of plant life which had been reduced to brown and decaying representatives of their former selves; she was in no hurry to remove these eyesores, although naturally, I was. I was outside, removing a dead plant hanging from the side of the house when I discovered there was a small bird nest tucked away in the center. Unfortunately, small holes in each of the otherwise intact eggs led me to believe that some insects or another bird had destroyed the embryos. There was a small plastic stick in the soil with a date scribbled on it. My thought was that Shari had made a notation about the eggs to track their progress, which I found very thoughtful and sweet. When she came home from work that evening, I gently approached her with the bad news.

"I was removing that dead plant hanging over the deck, and I found your bird nest. I don't know if you knew this already, but the eggs have been ruined."

She looked at me somewhat dumbstruck and said, "What plant? What nest?"

I couldn't believe it. I took her outside and showed her the plant I had taken down and set aside on a table. As reality was sufficiently squashing my sentimental misconception, I then said, "You've got to be kidding me! You mean to tell me that this plant has been hanging out here long enough for it to die, some bird to build a nest, lay eggs, have the eggs destroyed and this is the first you've heard of it!?" I then continued, "I thought the sticker in the plant was you acknowledging the eggs!" Shari gave a little laugh and said, "You give me too much credit."

Undoubtedly, one of the funniest memories we had actually involved Shari and her mother discussing gay relationships. Shari's mother asked her daughter one day to clarify how gay men differentiate each other's roles in relationships. Shari went on to explain that gay men used the terminology "top" and "bottom" to describe which partner plays the more dominant role, and which one plays the more subservient role. Shari's mother, obviously unaware of these role assignments, went on to ask if the same rules applied to lesbians. Shari said that although we generally adhere to the same idea in theory, we do not use the same terminology, but rather just distinguish ourselves as "femme" or "butch" or some variation thereof, which indicates (for the most part) which partner assumes which role. Out of fun curiosity, Shari asked her mother for her opinion on who she thought was more dominant in our relationship. Her mother replied, "Christine is on the top." Shari couldn't contain her laughter, and when her mother realized her mistake, she asked that Shari not share the exchange with me out of embarrassment, but of course Shari did. We would reference this joke innumerable times throughout the course of our relationship.

My two favorite phrases to say to Shari were "Anything for you" and "I adore you". The first time I told Shari that I adored her, she found it very striking and profound; when she was making her list of attributes she was looking for in an ideal mate prior to us ever meeting, she specifically stated that she wanted a lover that would "adore" her. (There are no coincidences, you know.) The other phrase, "Anything for you", taught us both a lesson in sincerity and sacrifice. I make it a point to select my words very carefully and deliberately, and I had told Shari that with the exceptions of doing harm to another living being or giving up my dogs, there wasn't anything I wouldn't do, give or attempt for her safety or happiness, and I meant those words, genuinely. I think the mass majority of people like to believe that they would do anything for their partner. People can assume, project or challenge the hypothetical all they like, but in an instant, actions will always speak louder than words; those actions will boldly reveal your priorities, values and true heart's desires. I unwaveringly believe this to be true.

Through the course of our relationship I went to Atlanta far more often than Shari came to Chicago; it was more convenient. Shari had her own place, and I could stay longer than she would have been able to anyway, because I was able to take some work with me. I would always drive so that I could have my two small dogs, Pepper and Nikita, come with me. It was more than a ten-hour drive, but I didn't mind in the least. I never complained, and never thought anything of it, honestly; I actually enjoyed it. Shari was utterly astounded by this, and told me so on many occasions.

"I've dated women in the past that weren't motivated enough to drive across the city to come and see me, let alone state lines!" Shari exclaimed.

That idea struck me as so sad and unbelievable. What could I say?
What I would always say:

"Anything for you."

Through Bad Times...

Remember what Fergie says: no matter how bad it gets,
"Big Girls Don't Cry."

Despite what some may think, I'm no princess.

I think as a rule people generally try to downplay their faults, particularly when dating. I am very open about my shortcomings, but I had gone so far as to list them on my online dating profile. I wish more individuals would be more forthcoming, don't you? We could expedite things so much quicker, wouldn't you agree? Of course everyone is trying to sell themselves, and wants to put on their best face, but I want to know the worst of it: the REAL deal. Tell me what I can really expect, not what your "representative" has to say.

My more undesirable traits are that I am sarcastic, impatient, vain, critical, demanding, overly-analytical, and often too blunt in my speech. I sometimes come across very confident which I have been told can be intimidating and off-putting. I bore easily and have a short attention span if a subject (or person) doesn't interest me. If I am particularly engaged in a discussion, I have a tendency to dissect the topic down to its atomic structure, which requires a certain cerebral endurance that I have only seen a handful of other individuals possess. I am admittedly hard to impress.

Okay, so maybe I'm a *little bit* of a princess.

My lover, Shari, on the other hand was extremely cluttered and disorganized, admittedly naïve, unpredictably moody and sporadically crass much like an adolescent boy.

How did we last as long as we did??

We were so vastly different: she was reserved, while I was outgoing. With strangers I was vigilant, while she had a tendency to be overly trusting. I was very passionate and she was at times…present.

We grated on one another: I despised her high-pitched sneezes and she disliked the way I would cut vegetables. I abhorred her tendencies to procrastinate, and she began to loathe my need to organize everything.

I was a nit-picking, egotistical Libra and she was a manic, Jeckyll-and-Hyde Gemini; what the hell were those astrology books talking about, "good match"??

When I told her that she was the closest thing to perfection I had ever found in a mate, she was offended by it: she wanted to know what she was lacking.

When couples argue, there will always be three versions to the situation: one partner's version, the other partner's version and the truth. I believe when the relationship is embroiled in turmoil, what each partner should strive for is to hear and understand the other partner, with the inevitable goal being to reach a compromise, if not an outright resolution. I myself am a firm believer in compromise.

I am happy to say that fights between the two of us were never ugly, violent or even disrespectful. There was never any name calling, no breaking of objects and no crew from the TV show *Cops* videotaping our escapades on the front lawn. Our "fights" consisted mainly of lengthy, disheartening conversations, which would on occasion, leave us at a stalemate. I'm embarrassed to admit that I think we hung up on one another a few times.

I read once somewhere that high in the hierarchy of why couples split up is the interference of other people, namely family members, i.e.

"in-laws". Although I believe this potential detriment should not be minimized, there is another issue that will take precedent...

It has been said that the number one thing that couples fight about (and inevitably breakup about) is money. I whole-heartedly believe this. We have experienced the discomfort surrounding this issue firsthand. Relationship experts would most likely dissuade a potentially new couple on opposite ends of the financial spectrum from proceeding because it can prove too stressful for the relationship. Both parties have to be very patient, considerate of their partner and crystal clear on the objectives of the relationship.

So Shari would on occasion hurt my feelings when it came to money (or my lack thereof) and I would on occasion hurt her feelings when it came to cleanliness (or her lack thereof.)

My lover's primary complaint of me was that I was indeed too critical. If I didn't like something, I let it be known, even if it was in *her* house. More than once I was guilty of using the term "disgusting" to describe a situation or thing that I found...well, disgusting! We discussed this on a few occasions and I did apologize sincerely. In certain instances I left her feeling inadequate, and she certainly did not deserve that. She was absolutely right. After having heard her out, I did make improvements to police my behavior. In a humorous attempt to justify my behavior though, I would go on to say that the editor (in my head) had "quit the staff", therefore leaving me susceptible to releasing sometimes offensive material to the masses. Her secondary complaint of me was that I did not "like" her mother and that I was not "family oriented" enough, failing to display adequate interest in her toddling nieces (or their uninteresting parents, for that matter.) I argued, "I *like* your mother just fine. But that is the extent of it!" I do admit that I do have a preference for animals over children, and do not get particularly giddy at the thought of babysitting others' offspring: after the first round of poopy diapers and screaming tantrums, their charm dissipates rather quickly.

My primary complaint of Shari was that I frequently felt a lack of genuine emotional support from her. Sometimes you only get one chance to not only say the right thing but also say it at the right time; I believe that when you are in the process of a deep verbal exchange with someone, sometimes it's not only the content of your response but the *timing* of your response that can make all the difference. Timing does matter (as demonstrated by all those hilarious TV commercials making light of the distress and misinterpretation caused by "dropped" cell phone calls!) We experienced this phenomenon on several awkward occasions, which was only made worse by the fact that we were face to face, and not on the phone!

The other unsettling issue with Shari was that she could at times become quite the adolescent boy, which absolutely astounded me! Here is a professional, successful woman in her mid-thirties who thought it was "funny" to buy a t-shirt that read "Nice legs…What time do they open?" Granted, the shirt is somewhat amusing, but am I dating some frat boy or the star from *Jackass*?? I had asked her, "Where do you intend to wear that?" as I thought to myself, "Nowhere *with me*, that's for damn sure!" (She actually ended up throwing the t-shirt away despite my best attempts to convince her to donate the shirt to a clothing collection drop box, where it might have made some underprivileged man's day.) Another time Shari had made one particularly explicit and too-vulgar-to-repeat remark about our sex life to one of her friends which just left me shaking my head in disbelief and finding the whole episode… "disgusting".

During the last summer, when we were still a couple, Shari and I had what was probably one of our most passionate disagreements, which surprisingly enough didn't deal with finances or third-party interference in our relationship; it also ironically resulted in one of our best resolutions. The argument was regarding some of our former lovers' personal effects that we both still had in our possession. I was completely willing to part with any memoirs that made Shari uncomfortable, although Shari on the other hand, was fighting tooth and nail against discarding anything. This wasn't an issue about insecurity in the least; these were relationships that had long been over. There was a principal involved (in my eyes) but no ultimatums were ever issued by either one of us. I remember the frustration of trying to make her understand my point of view, and attempting to conjure up a solution. I did in fact come up with an idea, but I thought it would have been considered too radical, so I stifled it, and patiently hoped that Shari would come up with some suggestions of her own. To my surprise, Shari did come up with an idea, which was the same idea I had: ceremoniously *burn* the items at the root of our dismay.

I appreciate that some people wouldn't agree with our decision, let alone understand it. We wanted a respectful way to acknowledge our past relationships before letting them go once and for all; we didn't want to simply throw any of our remnants in the garbage, because that was certainly no way to memorialize those who had been special in our lives at one time. This was a way for us to recognize that these previous relationships were important to us in the past, but now we had to make room for the new. We went to a local home improvement store, and Shari had bought a decorative, metallic firebowl for the occasion. I remember us being in the backyard and putting our effects inside the bowl while Shari started the fire. We silently held hands while watching the flames contagion. It wasn't sad or regretful for me in the least and I confessed to my lover as she stood beside me that I felt a satisfying feeling of calm mixed with relief to which she agreed.

Day Six: Group Therapy

It can't be wrong to search other people for answers ...
After all, Sarah Mclaughlan does in "Aidia" ...

Today I got together with Tara and Amy for breakfast; we also used this opportunity to meet Amy's new love interest, Rachel. It has actually been quite some time since I have seen Tara. Her recent ex-girlfriend did not like me *whatsoever*, solely based on my status as an "ex-girlfriend". (Remember my reference to security earlier?) This friction took an inevitable toll on our friendship. We have all been guilty of the same behavior at some point: we get involved in a new relationship and for whatever reason, friends become temporarily re-prioritized. I'm not condoning this practice, but everyone usually acknowledges the error of their ways in hindsight, and friendships are generally mended when that particular romantic relationship ends. I am happy to report, that Tara and I have resumed the warm friendship we had known previously.

I spoke to Shari this morning briefly. Part of our Sunday morning ritual when we are apart is to speak right after watching Joel Osteen on television. I absolutely adore Joel Osteen (along with a myriad of other motivational speakers) and I turned Shari on to the show in kind (after Amy turned me on to it.) She knew I was going out to breakfast, and we agreed to speak afterwards.

Tara met me at my family's house, so that we could have the thirty minute car ride to Amy's apartment to do some personal catching up. Tara had been running a little late, which was mildly taking a toll on Amy's nerves, because her anally-retentive metabolism was making her quite hungry. After a series of phone calls, I assured Amy that we were on the way.

Tara and I embarked on our journey, and within that thirty minute window, I had succinctly summarized the failures of my relationship with Shari. I painted for Tara a vivid picture of the situation at hand, and outlined my disastrous encounters with my (once upon a time) future pseudo-mother-in-law.

My romantic relationship with Tara had lasted three years, and ended nearly four years ago. She is a very attractive woman with a medium build, long curly dark hair and even darker eyes; strangers would mistake us more frequently for relatives than lovers. Tara's downfall is that she isn't the best decision maker: she prefers her lovers to "take the lead", as was the case when we were a couple (because as everyone knows, I'm "on the top".) Tara knows me well, and has the ability to be surprisingly unbiased in her analysis of me. I couldn't wait to hear what she had to say about this whole mess.

For starters, she thought the topic of the whole boundary-crossing mother issues was "weird". She commended me for offering a variety of compromises, and included particular accolades for suggesting a therapist to mediate. Tara sympathized with my lack of good options and appreciated my attempts to save this relationship, because let's face it: good lesbian relationships are hard to find! Seriously, to start, you only have a small percentage of the population to begin with that is authentically "lesbian" (not bi-sexual, and not caught up in some attention-seeking trend) and once you start narrowing down geographic considerations and implementing your own "must have" criteria, you aren't left with much to pick from! (Lower my standards you say? Never!) Having felt better for getting some direct feedback, I then started to inquire about the details of *her* sorted love life. Tara is in love with a significantly older woman, Lori, who is twenty years her senior.

We were now too close to Amy's apartment for me to hear the entirety, but we paused the story, and I would get the remaining details on the ride back to my house.

I was very happy for Amy to have met Rachel. Amy actually recently called off her engagement to her fiancé because she felt she couldn't suppress her homosexuality any longer, and this was her first "official" girlfriend. She has had a few lesbian encounters in her past, but never anyone "special". I met Amy not too long before I met Shari, so she had been privy to many developing details in my romance-gone-awry. Amy could best be described as "cute"; she is a very tall, thin woman with long wavy hair the color of a taffy apple. Some might consider her as gangly; unfortunately, she is also extremely clumsy, which is a characteristic she admits to quite readily. Despite our differences, there has always been a special connection between the two of us which caused us to get along famously.

We all met at Amy's apartment at 9:30 a.m., exchanged brief introductions and drove to Andersonville in Amy's car. For those that don't know, Andersonville is a trendy, lesbian laden neighborhood nestled on the North side of the city. It was a beautiful spring day in Chicago and when we arrived at the popular French bistrot, La Tache, I realized that I appreciate the sophisticated, vintage style of this restaurant more each time. I recommended that we eat at La Tache not only because I prefer to patronize gay/ lesbian owned establishments when at all possible, but the brunch there is quite phenomenal!

When we were all comfortably situated in a booth, I made the informal announcement that I was anxious to get the group's input on my relationship situation. Everyone was aware of everyone else's situation (through me) but Tara and Amy had asked me to not publicly divulge certain details of their own situations. Rachel was having certain family issues of her own, and didn't feel qualified to weigh in on the matter at hand.

Amy's new love interest was an attractive, petite woman with heaps of long, curly, blond hair, a fit body and a nice tan. Amy unofficially forewarned me in advance that Rachel was very "bubbly", and what this translates into is that she giggles at *everything* that is the least bit entertaining! I must have said five different sentences that elicited five different giggles from the woman which prompted me to glance at Tara; Tara responded to me with a discreet yet firm look which all at once said "I know what you're thinking and I agree, but don't you dare say a word!"

Rachel is almost 40 years old and has just "come out" to her family. Although the mother confronted Rachel with her suspicions years ago (which were denied) this news has been quite shocking, and to say that Rachel's mother is not taking it well would be an understatement. We all sympathized with Rachel because "coming out" is really something that you should be experiencing in your early twenties or late teens. I suppose it is comparable to what they say about having chicken pox: it is more desirable to have the affliction when you are younger, I think more for the sake of just getting it over and done with. Sometimes adults can be worse than children (case in point.)

Amy and Tara proceeded to take opposing views on my situation with Shari. Tara said I should give it up and find someone else worthy of my affection, while Amy (much like myself, the little optimist) thought that breaking up over someone's mother and some other minor issues were not good enough reasons to throw in the proverbial towel, and that I should hang in there. Although normally I would agree whole-heartedly, I reminded her that if the other party is not inclined to work on the couple's problems, then it really is futile. (Did I just answer my own question?)

I had brought three pictures to the restaurant of a dinner I had gone to with Shari and her mom from months past. I only recently acquired these pictures on my last trip to Atlanta. Two of the pictures were of Shari and me, side by side, looking very "coupley". The third picture was of me and Shari's mom, side by side and unintentionally looking very "coupley" as well. No one was impressed by Shari's pictures, and it was obvious that they were trying their best to *delicately* insult her appearance. Granted, they weren't the best pictures, but I didn't think I looked that much better myself. Everyone could agree though that my breasts were looking particularly perky in one of the pictures. (Well, it is a table of women, and remember, gay or straight, women will *always* make scrutinizing observations about other women. Even if they never say a word aloud, trust me, they are scrutinizing!) At that junction, Tara commented on one of the pictures, saying that we really "are a cute couple". Seconds later the joke is revealed that the reference was made to the picture of me and *Shari's mom*! That resulted in a brief uproar of laughter from our table.

The rest of the time was spent touching on each other's various issues and conundrums at hand, to the extent that each was comfortable releasing their own edited versions. I was marveling at the distinctly different mini-dramas each of us had, and remarked that we had our own little episode of the *L Word* going on! I proposed that perhaps I should contact their writers.

Rachel spoke a little about her family and her nieces that she adores. Tara and I then learned a little factoid about Rachel's three-year-old niece who innocently references female genitalia as "china"; Rachel and Amy now make the same playful reference between one another. At that very moment Tara felt compelled to reference her own girlfriend, Lori, and very proudly proclaimed, "I got myself some *fiiine* china!" Anxious to repay her for her earlier joke on me, I responded, "Giiiirrrl, you got yourself some *antique* china!" Our table was again in an uproar of laughter. Tara struggled for a witty comeback, but came up empty-handed this round. Meanwhile I was mildly concerned that the restaurant management was going to reprimand us for our raucous behavior, and I was not relishing the thought of a public scolding.

We left the restaurant, returned back to Amy's apartment and Tara and I left promptly from there. Amy and Rachel didn't have much time together, because Rachel was only visiting for the weekend (and it was apparent that they had other things on their agenda!)

Tara used the ride back to my house as the opportunity to finish catching me up on the web of her own personal romantic drama which now has her entangled. It would appear that Lori, Tara's love interest, is not *entirely* broken up with her own lover of twenty years. The excuses that Lori offers are plentiful, and understandable, given the codependent nature of that specific relationship. Lori has been the caretaker in her twenty-year relationship, and face it, who doesn't like to be needed? This unfortunately puts Tara in the unofficial position of "the other woman." I listen, I offer advice, and I know that my observations will not impact Tara at all. Like the rest of us, Tara knows what she has to do, but just has to be moved to the point of action in her own time.

I called Shari very quickly when I had returned to my family's house with Tara, simply to tell her that Tara would be visiting for a bit, and that I would call her soon. Shari inquired how breakfast was, and asked for a quick overview. After providing her with a synopsis, she said that our outing sounded much like a lesbian support group, which I guess, wasn't entirely off the mark! That makes me think that perhaps we have all participated in more "group therapy" than we were ever even aware of, we just did it under the guise of enjoying mimosas and crepes. As Shari and I were getting off of the phone I was slightly disappointed to hear that she had chore-related "things to do" and that she would prefer to just speak at our normal time, which was before bed. I agreed and hung up the phone again feeling somewhat sad. Tara witnessed the transformation as I relayed what had just happened; she sympathized with me and agreed that was "crappy".

My mom and stepfather were elated to see Tara again. My mother admits that Tara was always her personal favorite. My dogs were absolutely beside themselves with glee upon seeing her again. We all conversed in the family room for awhile, before Tara and I decided to take the dogs for a walk at the park just down the street.

It really was a picture perfect day outside, and it was quite enjoyable to be spending time with a woman who is much more a good friend, than an ex-girlfriend. We agreed that our relationship is not the norm, but that makes it all the more precious to me. We spent a little more time discussing our dilemmas and a little time reminiscing about our past together. After about an hour we started to bring the dogs back to the house, because we both had things that needed to get done today.

We said our goodbyes and I began my attempts at productivity, trying to shake off the residue of my earlier conversation with Shari. I felt a strange sense of resolution as I began to accept that not speaking or communicating with Shari any longer (at least for quite some time) might be best for all involved. (A real epiphany, right?)

A few hours went by and the phone rang: it was Shari. I was not in a position to answer the phone at that moment, so I let it go to voicemail. After I had seen it was her calling, I admittedly took my time in returning her call, debating whether I should let even more time elapse (yes, out of spite.)

In true "Drama Queen" fashion, I called her back and immediately notified her of the distress she had caused me, both last night and today. She apologized and acknowledged her contributions to my distress. (I was always very appreciative of her accountability; that is one of the things I love about her.) An hour long conversation ensued which basically brought to light her indecision on how best to deal with our situation. She was not relishing the thought of addressing the situation with her mother, whatsoever. I challenged her to find another girlfriend that would be so compromising and determined to resolve such differences. Find that woman that will fight for a relationship so adamantly (and when you do find her, I said, please give her my number!) After much of the same dialogue that has taken place for six days now, I declared that it was best if we did not speak anymore in any context until (if or when) the time came that she has had her *own* epiphany. She needed to bring something to the table. I was tired of being the proverbial cheerleader of this relationship, and I was hereby putting my pom-poms down as of this very moment! I cautioned her that although this was not an ultimatum, per se, this train would be pulling out of the station for good, unless she actually made some kind of contribution to the situation which would stop its otherwise irrevocable outcome. To this declaration I received a most lackluster "okay" which signified that we could now at least begin *acting* like a couple that was broken up.

We got off of the phone, and I was more relieved than sad at that moment.

Day Seven: Dream Interpretation

The band Goldfinger is with me, "Still Counting the Days"...

I woke up at 4:30 a.m. this morning after having a very disturbing dream. I dreamt that I was sitting on the edge of a bed with a very frail and elderly woman when suddenly she started having a terrible coughing fit. This was the kind of coughing fit that was so violent that she started to throw up. I was rubbing her back and trying to get her to calm down. She fell to the floor on her hands and knees between the bed and the nightstand. I was considering calling 911, because she was just becoming more and more agitated, and the coughing was not subsiding. She had actually crawled under the bed, towards the headboard. I got on the floor and was trying to coax her out from under there, so I could help. The last visual I was left with was of this pathetic looking old woman's face, tongue sticking out, in mid-cough ... then I woke up. I was very upset by this and instantly sprang into deep analysis, because we all know, there was no going back to sleep after that one!

After much concentrated thought, I made a connection: whenever Shari's dog, Boomer, would get sick, he would crawl under her bed to throw up. His favorite place to loiter (and go hide when he was in trouble) was under the bed, *under the headboard.* Good Lord, now I'm even dreaming about *her dog*?!

I sent off an email to Amy in the next hour, because I knew she was up (and probably reading her email.) Then I sent the same email to a friend of ours, Karen, who I do not believe ever sleeps. Amy sent me a quick and silly reply, "You really should stop smoking that stuff." Very funny. I did get a more appropriate response a little later from her, stating that she interpreted it as representative of my dying relationship with Shari.

The reason I sent the email to Karen is because Karen is a unique individual that some might even coin "eccentric" (and I think this puzzle-solving is right up her alley!) Remember that TV show *Martin*? Remember Martin's friend Tommy that had a mysterious occupation that nobody could actually claim to know? Karen would be Tommy's female counterpart: nobody knows what the hell she does professionally besides "this and that" but she does lead a very full and adventurous life, complete with world travels and much social activity (but I think that her being a native of the Dominican Republic has a lot to do with these points.) Life is never dull when Karen is around, as I have witnessed firsthand. One small aside: Karen is transgendered; she was born a man.

Karen actually left me a voicemail last night but I was negligent in returning her call, so sharing the dream with her gave me the opportunity to apologize for last night as well. Her voicemail was to tell me that I was right: her ex-girlfriend, Angel, that she had been aggressively attempting to reconcile with (for the past year) was playing her for a fool. Last fall I had met some of Karen's friends that knew Angel and they had confided in me that Angel was just *using* Karen for her anything she could get her little claws into: she was a master manipulator. I actually met Angel once and didn't care for her, but I'm sure that was because I knew her alleged background and was prone to believe it. Karen and I are not extremely close, but I care about her as a person, and do not want to see her get hurt, or be blatantly taken advantage of; we have discussed this situation on several occasions. Karen had been in a particularly good mood as of late, because supposedly Angel had come to her senses and was "coming home" back to Chicago to be with the love of her life. Uh-huh. Sure she is. In this morning's email to me came the revelation from Karen that she had discovered Angel's profile on an online dating site, *seeking men*. (This was not a surprise either, because the girl had been caught in bi-sexual escapades before by Karen.) How many times must we touch the hot stove before we learn? Hell, I think some of us have burnt off all of our proverbial digits, but will still offer up a palm or an elbow, just so we can touch that stove *one more time* (because you know, *this time* could be different!) Ignorance can certainly be blissful.

As far as Karen's interpretation of my dream goes, it is in the same vein as Amy's (except Karen gave a much lengthier, thorough translation of what all of the symbolism meant, right down to the vomit.) In sum: my relationship is dying, and there is a bunch of crap coming to the surface. Pretty accurate, I would say.

The morning progressed and I had to run some errands (I was staying busy, you know!) I did have a sentimental moment which caught me a bit off guard while listening to the radio in the car, though. The Chris Issac song "Wicked Game" came on (which is pretty depressing in itself) and I found myself paying attention to the lyrics a little *too closely*. Some talk of feelings, and dreaming…I immediately changed the station. Somehow that emotional stirring has drudged up the memory of my favorite embrace with Shari. Ugh! Must stop! Must stop!

Amy and I chatted throughout the day via email, text message and lunchtime phone conversation; she was keeping me abreast of the situation between Rachel and Rachel's mother. Bookies in Vegas are figuring the odds of how long this relationship between Amy and Rachel will actually last with a meddling mother right in the middle. (Case in point.)

I had been looking at the pictures that I brought to breakfast yesterday of my former lover. I had to admit, those pictures did not do her justice at all! What was most disturbing to me though was the fact that I could look at those pictures without a deep sense of loss…it wasn't as bothersome as I would expect. Was I getting over it? Was I over it? Or was I in denial?

I've wondered on and off today if I will ever hear from Shari again. Today it had been a week since our breakup, almost to the hour (but who's counting?) We have had no form of contact whatsoever since yesterday, and honestly, it is a little strange. I checked my personal email a few times, not expecting to hear from her, but maybe secretly hoping she had sent me something. Would she come to her senses? She wasn't really going to let this relationship end, would she? We were practically engaged, for God's sake (or as engaged as two women could be, under the extent of our current law!)

The ball was clearly in her court and it was out of my hands. If she was at peace with the notion of throwing away everything in the face of some minor relationship challenges, then fine; it was her loss. I was obviously better off without her...

It would be nice to hear from her, though.

Day Eight: Shock and Awe

Come on now, after all of this breaking up and making up,
Al Green and I are utterly confused! "Let's Stay Together"!

I woke up later than I would have liked this morning; this has been happening the past few days because I am staying up a little longer than usual keeping this journal. This does not make me happy. I enjoy being an "early to bed, early to rise" kind of girl, and the one to two hour difference is ruining my discipline. Well, as long as I am ruining my discipline, I decided I might as well have a piece of chocolate cake for breakfast. I am now embracing the idea of "self-medicating" to expedite my healing process, and chocolate is my medicine of choice.

This morning I had a new business strategy and I had sent my brainstorm off to Amy in an email. I was getting ready to make a run to Starbucks and stopped momentarily to exchange morning pleasantries with my mother in the kitchen (and also take the opportunity to run the business idea past her as well.)

Our conversation was interrupted by my cell phone ringing, which I assumed was Amy, weighing in on the topic at hand (and displaying impeccable timing.) Surprise overtook me at that moment: it was Shari! (My mom rolled her eyes.)

I took the call as I headed out the door. "What are you doing?" she asked. "Getting ready to grab some coffee. What are you doing?" I replied.

"Calling you" she said. ("Isn't that cute" I thought. She is incorporating my witty replies.) We spoke for the ten minutes that it took me to drive to my destination.

She wanted to know if we could speak tonight. I assured her we could. She had some time to think about things and thanked me for giving her the room to do so. Truth be told here: I wasn't "giving her time"; I was under the impression it was really over. I never expected to hear from her again. Another one of our major differences is that I react instantaneously to various stimuli, unlike Shari, who likes to take her time and really contemplate her responses. This drives me insane. I believe that a person's initial reaction to something is most times their most honest one. Please, do not sanitize or edit what you were going to say for the sake of being PC! What I want is truth (and the more promptly, the better!)

I did take a minute to ask her how she was handling other parties' incoming text messages. I had noticed that since our "breakup" I had been particularly sensitive to the sound of my text messages, and automatically assumed it was her (which it had been 98% of the time in the past.) She said she became sad and annoyed when she received texts from other people, because she hoped it was me, and reacted like some kind of lovesick Pavlovian dog! She would prefer other people not text message her while we work through our differences. I, on the other hand, encouraged people to text me, in light of the recent events, to desensitize myself to the melodic notification…assuming we really are breaking up, of course!

She was getting ready to walk into work, and I was sitting in the parking lot of Starbucks. The conversation had been pleasant, and I began to get off of the phone warmly, albeit a little more casually than usual which I believed was appropriate, given the circumstances. There was a pause followed by her saying "I miss you." I reciprocated the sentiment and then I attempted to get off of the phone again; this time she inserted "I love you." Oh! That caught me a little off guard, not because I doubted it, but I was still in a little bit of shock that we were even speaking to begin with! I told her that I loved her too, and we hung up, agreeing to speak again at our "usual" time in the evening.

In the afternoon I received an email from Amy telling me that the situation between Rachel and her family seemed to be coming to a head. Rachel's mother was now wielding guilt (and tears) as weapons, as only a maternal gladiator could. Rachel had become an object of shame to the family and her mother was now literally crying to Rachel's sisters about…about what? Did Rachel's sisters know she's a lesbian? If not, did her mom tell them? Rachel doesn't even know! Yes, let's complicate this matter a little further by not knowing exactly what everyone else knows! What a mess!

I ended up sending Shari a text saying that I was very shocked that she called. A few hours later I received a return text saying that she was surprised that I was shocked.

By the time evening came, I was not especially looking forward to our phone call. Shari sounded enthusiastic, while I sounded and felt somewhat distant. I was very preoccupied with work thoughts, and it probably wasn't the best time to be discussing our situation.

I do not have the patience for vagueness, and vague was how Shari was coming across initially. She wanted to "work it out." I unleashed a barrage of questions: How does she propose we "work it out"? What happened to her bad instinctual feelings? She's had this time to think, so what exactly did she think about? My tone is putting her off. She thought this may not be the time to discuss things, and she may have been right, but we were embroiled, so let's finish it. At one point I admittedly became sarcastic and asked "you were the one that had to go and think, so what did you bring back from the mountaintop with you?" (What a beast I could be! I deserve my own beastie character in the children's book *Where the Wild Things Are!*)

She began by saying that after some contemplation, she realized that we had more that was good in our relationship than more that was bad. She accepted responsibility for some previous pain she had caused me, and apologized for that. She said we could use some therapy to address the issue of her mother so that I don't feel "overwhelmed" and her mother doesn't feel...I offer the word "neglected" and she agreed. Her agreement to my term just caused a wave of illness to pass over me briefly. I have really had enough needy women in my lifetime, and this arrangement didn't sound like a very enticing offer after all.

I told her I needed to think about it.

She confessed that she was surprised. With as impulsive as I am, I really don't do much mulling over anything. This one I would, though. In my mind our relationship (which had been on life support) was in cardiac arrest, and we had to jump in and perform CPR right now or just let nature take its course.

I definitely needed to think about it.

She understood but requested that I let her know either way what my decision would be, when I came to it. We agreed to speak "later" and said goodnight.

I was exhausted and just wanted to go to bed.

Day Nine: Back and Forth

I will bend ... and bend ... and bend some more until
I snap into pieces ... Luckily the band Stained will be
"Right Here" to help put me back together ...

From the time I went to bed last night, to the time I woke up this morning I had been reflecting on my conversation with Shari. (What a surprise.) For the first time, the ball was in *my* court. I had consistently lobbied for this relationship, and now, I just didn't know if it was really what I wanted after all. Maybe my friends were right: maybe I was suffering from the syndrome of merely wanting what I couldn't have ...

I was tempted to call her to say "Good morning". Something instinctively told me that that was not a good idea, either because it would become the catalyst that sucked me back into a situation which I was not entirely convinced I wanted to be sucked back into, or that she would be not-so-receptive due to my cold front last night.

To call, or not to call? *That* is the question! To Hell with it! I'll call! After all, today may be the day that bus has my name on it!

Shari was surprised to be hearing from me in light of last night's awkwardness, but claimed that it was a "pleasant surprise." (Unlike it's counterpart, the occasionally experienced "horrified surprise", like the time Shari moved her refrigerator in order to investigate a foul smell in the kitchen to find a dead mouse half engulfed in an electric socket.)

The call went better than expected. She was getting ready for work and took a few minutes to talk to me, which I always appreciated. We compared maladies and she told me that the apparent stress of the situation had made her break out in a horrible rash of adult acne, while I complained that my stomach had been quite rebellious for the past week. We got off the phone shortly thereafter, agreeing to speak again at lunchtime, during her break which was part of our usual routine.

About twenty minutes passed and I knew that she was driving to work, so I took the opportunity to call her back. I shared with her my mild disappointment that she did not offer to call me on her drive to work, as was also our usual ritual. She apologized, and claimed that had she known I wanted to talk, she certainly would have called me. Obviously, she did not want to overstep any boundaries. We used this opportunity to talk about mostly irrelevant things, just for the sake of "catching up." We got off the phone warmly, and confirmed that we would be speaking during the lunch hour.

The time that elapsed between our morning call and our afternoon call had given me ample opportunity to drudge up many doubts about the situation, so by the time Shari called, I was quite skeptical about the whole predicament.

This afternoon call was not supposed to be particularly in depth, or the time for heavy conversation, but it was quickly headed this way, as I voiced concerns about our going to therapy. My main concern was that although Shari had (reluctantly) agreed to go, I was afraid that she would not be receptive to what the therapist had to say in terms of her mother's role in our relationship. Frankly, I had yet to see Shari stand up to her mother, and I doubted if she could do it now. As the conversation wore on, it was apparent that it was taking a dark turn. Shari's tone began to change. I told her it sounded to me as though she truly didn't want to go to therapy. She agreed; she did *not* want to go to therapy. She accused me of only wanting to see a therapist so that a third party could validate my theory that the problem was all her mother, or her and her mother together. She said I presented myself as faultless and did not acknowledge my part in contributing to the problem. Realistically, I had to agree: I *did* believe that her mother was the majority of the problem.

Somewhat angrily, she said she would mail me my things promptly. This relationship was over.

Over the next two hours I contemplated what had elapsed. Well, we *almost* got back together; we seemed to have taken the proverbial one step forward, fell into a pothole, and broke a leg. I began questioning whether or not there is any truth to what she had said. Was I being unfair? Was I giving Shari the benefit of the doubt? I didn't think I was, and I concluded that that was *not* fair.

I sent her a text message apologizing for my accusatory tone, deeming her incapable of being receptive to therapy. I asked if we could speak after work. The reply came "Girl, you are fixin' to drive me crazy." Well, that wasn't very clear to me, so I sent the question "yes or no?" She responded by saying we could speak tonight and thanked me for the apology.

Instead of calling her at the usual time, I called Shari as soon as she had gotten out of work to confirm that our later conversation was going to be a good one. I mean, if we were merely going to converse for her to tell me that this wasn't going to work after all, then why wait another two hours? Let's just get it over with. She stated that that was not her intention, and we could anticipate a normal (or at the very least, a status quo) phone call.

In about another two hours we were speaking again. (We really did speak frequently, but I believe it was partially due to the distance between us; things may have been different had we been able to see one another more regularly, but then again ...) We were discussing our discussion from earlier. Only women can discuss discussions. She was physically and emotionally tired, and it was apparent. I suggested that we utilize a friendly acquaintance of mine, Margot, as an initial mediator to give us some preliminary feedback on the situation. Margot, although a practicing counselor, was not a licensed or a degreed "professional", but would be able to undoubtedly shed some light on the situation; she worked primarily as an "intuitive". Shari was mostly interested in Margot's opinion as to whether or not it would really be necessary to incorporate Shari's mother into the therapy and at what point, because to say the Shari was not looking forward to that segment of the program would be a gross understatement! We came to that agreement that I would set a phone session up with Margot, with one condition: Shari (at the very least) would tell her mother tomorrow when they met for breakfast that we were *considering* getting back together and looking into therapy. She agreed, but wanted to break the news to her mother in "stages." First we would introduce the idea of a possible reconciliation, then perhaps we could mention therapy, and finally we would (ever so delicately) ask her mother to partake in the process.

It was painfully evident that Shari really was not in a chatty mood. She claimed that part of her emotional "sagginess" was partially because she was tired, but also because she felt so "disconnected" from me. Something had "died in our relationship" and for the first time she had the stark realization from talking to me last night that our relationship might *actually* be ending. I wondered to myself: could we ever, EVER be on the same page at the same time? We ended up hanging up the phone in a way that left me feeling rather distraught.

I called Amy who was eating a late-night snack and watching *South Park* (both of which are highly unusual for Amy.) I started picking on a few dark-chocolate covered cookies myself. She barely had time to tell me of the silliness that was unfolding on the television when my other line rang: it was Shari. I had let Amy go and in the process of switching lines, I accidentally hung up on Shari. The phone rang again (which I was assuming was a call back) and when I answered, I apologized for the mishap. Shari didn't understand what had transpired because there was no technical mishap on her end. As I tried to explain further, she cut in and asked "Can we stop long enough for me to just tell you I love you? I wanted to get off the phone in a better way." I agreed most certainly. With that being said, I could go to bed now feeling better than I had in at least nine days.

The Wisdom of Strangers

We could really use a good talking to from Brad Paisley, although he would probably just end up telling us "All You Really Need Is Love…"

Having spent so much time in Atlanta, I came to the sad realization that eventually I was going to have to find a new hair stylist. I was not looking forward to this task, for I had already tried the salon that Shari went to and found them to be not only overpriced but also offering very poor service. I decided to take a risk and visit a salon that was right next door to a local restaurant in Roswell that Shari and I liked to have breakfast at on occasion. I was on a mission: my hair was rather long, and despite Shari's objections, I was determined to have it cut.

The shop was called About Hair. When I walked inside, I realized the salon was very small yet quaint, and possessed a certain charm and energy that notified me that I was in the company of good people. No one was at the front desk when I arrived, but there was a woman in her late fifties seated in one of the stylist's chairs closest to the front door with her head saturated in coloring dye, and wearing a stylist's cape. She had been engrossed in conversation with some other ladies but when she had seen me, she walked over to greet me.

"May I he'p you?" She asked with the most adorable Southern drawl I think I had ever heard in my life.

I explained to the woman that I was new in the area and was wondering if there was someone available who could cut my hair, given the short notice. I was quite surprised when she stated that *she* could help me, and that I could just follow her. Admittedly, I was nervous about having a much older woman cut my hair. Surely, our generational gap would prove a challenge, and how on earth could I explain to her what I wanted without even having a picture as an aid? I took a proverbial leap of faith.

After she washed my hair and I was seated in her chair, she asked me what I had wanted her to do. I had uttered maybe a maximum of three sentences of my attempt at a description, when she declared "I got it!" Now I was really nervous.

As she began cutting, we commenced with customary small talk. I learned that her name was Sheryl, and she had originally been the owner of the salon. She sold the business, but chose to stay on as a manager. She asked me various questions about where I was from (because obviously my Northern accent gave me away) and what brought me to town. I told her that I was involved in a long-distance relationship, and was careful to watch my pronoun usage and to be tactfully vague. She was delighted and intrigued to hear about my "significant other" and gave all indications that she assumed I was dating a man. I carefully delivered my responses, feeling somewhat uncomfortable that I was feeding into her assumptions.

When the haircut was over, I was elated! It was *exactly* what I had wanted! I praised her work unabashedly, trying to purge some of the guilt I was feeling about my discriminatory thoughts from earlier. I told her I would most certainly be back again.

That evening, I had gleefully discussed my initial experience at the salon with my girlfriend, who was genuinely happy that I had a pleasant experience (knowing how difficult I could be to please sometimes.) As a rule I do not throw out compliments flippantly, therefore when I do give one you can be certain that it is well deserved! Shari and I laughed at the fact that my girlfriend was mistaken for my "boyfriend" and we reveled in the irony. I told Shari that I was tempted to tell Sheryl the truth about our relationship; Shari suggested I exercise my own discretion because we were in the somewhat conservative suburbs of Atlanta, and after all, it was the South.

Now I was a little concerned.

Some months had passed and during one of my many visits back to Atlanta I was again in need of a haircut, so I did not hesitate to make an appointment with my new found friend, Sheryl.

Sitting again in the stylist's chair, with minimal instruction, Sheryl set to work on the mess that was my hair. I had already anticipated that our conversation would resume where we had left off since our last meeting, and I had made a conscious decision to tell her the truth about my orientation, should the topic arise. I did not have to wait long.

While Sheryl was parting strands of my wet hair with her comb, she began asking me how my "boyfriend" was doing, and if I was enjoying my visit. I actually thought to myself that it might be best to address this topic either immediately *before* she began cutting the hair or immediately *after* the haircut was finished just in case I was found to be so offensive that I would be asked to leave (and thus not be forced to endure a partially cut head of hair.) I decided the earlier the better.

"Sheryl," I began cautiously as I looked at her standing behind me in the mirror, "I would like to clear something up...I hope this won't impact our relationship because I really enjoy coming to your salon..."

She looked concerned. "What it is, Darlin'?"

"The person I'm seeing is actually a woman. I don't have a boyfriend; she is my girlfriend. I am a lesbian."

Sheryl put her hands on my shoulders, and to my surprise, began apologizing profusely for the misunderstanding!

I was quite relieved by her reaction and set to apologizing in turn for having misled her during our initial meeting. I explained that I was simply erring on the side of caution.

"Lemme tell you somethin'," she began. "My bes' friend, who I have known some twenty-sumpthin' years is a lesbian...and I couldn't love her more. It don' bother me a 'tall. Don' you worry."

I thanked her for her reassurance and soon asked, "What about you Sheryl? Now that you know about me...what about you? Is there anyone special in your life?" I gave her a little smile and wink in the mirror.

She shared with me that she had been married for just over twenty years and she lost her husband only three years ago in a horrible car accident. A few months ago she had just started to date a very nice gentleman, and was apparently content with the relationship's progression.

I expressed my condolences for her loss, but then shared my sincere happiness for her in finding someone to care for again. The gravity of her situation slowly made its presence known, and it struck me as very deep and profound. How do you go on after losing a partner you've been with for decades? And how do you ever date again?

"Wow, Sheryl. Twenty *years*? Couples today don't last twenty *months*! Hell, in Hollywood do they last twenty *hours*? I don't think they make relationships like that anymore" I joked. "What's your secret?"

Her following revelation struck me as particularly poetic not only by the conviction in her voice, but by the sweet Southern accent coating her words.

"Relationships ain't easy. They're work. You hafta work on it EVERY DAY. Now, sure as Hell there's gonna be days where you don' wanna work on it, but you hafta. It's like a job. I'm not sayin' it's always gonna be like that, 'cause you're gonna have good times and bad times, but you just *never* stop workin' on it."

When my haircut was finished, we hugged each other goodbye. I was anxious to get back to see Shari.

We had some work to do.

Day Ten: Getting Better

The boys of Nickelback know what I'm feeling:
I love her and I have loved her all the while,
no matter how "Far Away" she was ...

As far as I can remember, I have always had stomach problems. I've never had an ulcer or anything substantial, but rather an ongoing series on gastrointestinal maladies for years and years. I read once in a book by Louise Hay that our emotions dictate everything that happens to us physically, and that the problems I am having signify an inability to "stomach" some portion of this process. But which portion? Is the loss of this relationship making me ill, or the possibility of getting back together?

I had woken up this morning and felt sick. I had stomach cramps and was slightly nauseous. I thought some more dark-chocolate covered cookies would help make this subside. (Didn't tribes from ancient civilizations believe in the medicinal powers of chocolate? Who am I to argue with the wisdom of the elders from civilizations past?)

Shari was supposed to have breakfast with her mother this morning and break the news to her about our potential reconciliation. I am not expecting this to go particularly well after Shari's revelation last night that her mother thinks I am "not nurturing enough" for her daughter and that I am too "high maintenance." Actually, her exact words were that I am a "spoiled princess that always gets what she wants." (If this were in actuality the case, the woman would be on a cruise liner with a one-way ticket to Singapore!)

Shari called me on the way home from her breakfast with her mother. I was practically bursting with curiosity! Shari said within five minutes of sitting down, her mother suspected something because of Shari's unusually good mood. Shari's coy smiles to her mother's pointed questions confirmed everything. The cat was out of the bag. Shari confessed that we were working towards a resolution and that we were looking into therapy. Her mother didn't give Shari an argument, but did say in her opinion that we didn't need therapy. I was quite surprised by what happened next: Shari (allegedly) told her mother that she and I had actually been getting along rather well until our last fateful dinner date, so yes, perhaps we did need some therapy (or at the very least, some mediation.) Unfortunately what happened next did *not* surprise me: Shari's mother asked who was going to be paying for therapy. We ended the conversation shortly thereafter because we were both in the process of running errands and agreed to speak in a few hours.

Within the next hour I was venting to my own mother about the offense I felt as a result of in the inquiry made into the future therapy bill.

"That's none of her *Goddamn* business!" my mother angrily declared.

I had to laugh at the irony here: my mother was defensively weighing in on the subject of Shari's mother weighing in on the subject of the restoration of my relationship with Shari; perfect.

I put in a call to my friend Margot, and gave her an abbreviated version of the situation. She agreed that she would speak to each of us at a scheduled time for an hour each, and then she would speak to the both of us on a three-way call. This mini-session would determine whether we needed to continue to see a "professional" therapist, and also let us know if (in Margot's opinion) we would be able to resolve this situation without Shari's mother directly participating.

The next time I spoke to Shari it was late evening. I told her that I had spoken to Margot and had made a tentative appointment for my portion of the session. Shari was taken somewhat aback when I stated that the appointment was an hour for each of us, and (in not so many words) requested that we reduce it to half an hour each. (Obviously, this woman has never been to therapy. Once those floodgates open, you'd be amazed at how time flies!) I will oblige her, though, for the sake of compromise. She wanted me to make her appointment for her, immediately following mine (because she wanted me to be the one to tell Margot that "we" have decided to narrow it down to half an hour each.) I would do this for her as well. I was just elated by the progress we were making! Perhaps our ailing relationship is able to come off of life support and do a little breathing on its own …

Shari made a realization tonight that she wanted to share with me, but preceded the release of this information with a stipulation: I was not to use this revelation as weaponry in the future. I agreed and she was free to divulge her thought. Shari came to the conclusion, after ample reflection, that her mother really hadn't liked *any* of her past girlfriends, nor does she particularly like her current daughter-in-law. Shari wasn't sure if the pressuring I had been experiencing wasn't a result of her mother trying to compensate for the unfulfilling relationship she has had with her son's wife. I was not surprised by any part of this revelation, but was pleased with what appeared to be traces of objectivity in Shari.

I shared with my former lover that I was writing this very book about our breakup. She was not surprised. I also told her that I wished she had written her own account of the events, because I thought it would have been interesting and entertaining to see both sides of the same story, on the same timeline, being published simultaneously. Seeing as things were looking fairly positive for us recently, I wondered if we were headed for a reconciliation … which would mean the end of my manuscript…I had genuinely enjoyed keeping this journal and would be disappointed at ending my pet project so abruptly … It reminded me of that *Seinfeld* episode when Jerry has to decide whether he wants to continue to date the woman he'd been seeing, or forsake the relationship so that he can continue impersonating her stomach in a funny voice. Decisions, decisions.

Towards the end of this particular conversation with my former (but soon to be current again) lover, we were regaining some of our lusty playfulness. We started to recount various rendezvous with one another, which led to some very steamy conversation. Steamy conversation would undoubtedly lead to some steamy emails later (which will be saved in that "special" folder in my computer.) The one thing we have always had and never falters is our physical chemistry and attraction for one another and that makes me very happy.

As we were saying our goodbyes, I was taken aback somewhat by her parting: "I love you, I miss you and I want to make this relationship work."

I stated that I thought we were getting our re-connection back to which she agreed..

Day Eleven: Then a Right Hook

What is this, the "Sunday Morning" No Doubt sang about???

This morning I had the song by Daughtry stuck in my head, "It's Not Over." This was the first time in ten days that Shari and I were exchanging pleasant morning emails. We both were feeling and sounding a little bit more optimistic about the situation. She wrote "I feel as though a great weight has been lifted off of my shoulders." I shared Amy's cautionary mindset about my relationship though; I knew the problem with Shari's mother hadn't been rectified yet (note: see chapter entitled "B is for Breakup") and somewhat compared it to the calm before the storm. I tried not to read too much into it though, but rather pondered the situation lightly over a cup of coffee.

I had gotten word that Amy and Rachel's "mamma-drama" was calming down; Rachel's mother had (for the time being) aborted the anti-lesbian campaign. I couldn't help but wonder if that was a calm before another storm. That reminded me, I needed to check in with Karen and Tara to see how their situations were developing, as well.

Karen was in overdrive with post-breakup busyness of her own so she wouldn't be readily available for idle chatting for awhile. She is far too energetic for me, so I will wait for her to reach the brink of collapse to catch up with her more thoroughly later.

Tara told me that she and Lori have plans for a mini-getaway this weekend at a bed-and-breakfast nearby. A few days ago, Lori finally decided to break the news to her former lover of 20 years that she was severing their ties of codependency. From the sounds of it, Lori took it much harder than the partner she could not completely separate herself from. I hoped for Tara's sake that this ensuing closure between Lori and her ex doesn't affect their getaway this weekend.

Shari and I spoke briefly at the beginning of lunchtime and I gently broached the topic of our pre-breakup Easter weekend plans. The summary of our original plan was for me to housesit and watch her dog while she spent Easter with her family in Florida. I realize this may sound a little crazy, but while I didn't particularly care to spend the holiday weekend with her family, her mother probably wouldn't have wanted me to go anyway, and I didn't want to see Boomer boarded at the vet most importantly. My family didn't have any formal plans for Easter this year either, so I wouldn't have been missing much. We would both like to see our original plans through, but we both thought it was best to wait to see what our sample therapy session brings. I had already spoken with Margot a second time, and it was established that Shari and I would both be having our telephone sessions with Margot Monday evening.

Shari called me back on the way back to work following lunch about an hour later, and I could hear in her voice that something was wrong so I questioned her about it. She'd "been thinking"… (Here it comes.) She doesn't want to go to therapy. I asked her patiently what the main objection was: was it the money? Was it having to discuss our problems with a third party? Was it the fear of having to integrate her mother potentially at some point? Was it the fear of being forced to realize that there really is something unhealthy about this triad? What was it???

She stated "I just don't think it will work."

Well, how can I argue with logic like that?

If her mind was already made up, then I am sure it would *not* work. And *of course*, she continued, it is just silly to consider therapy given the fact that we have a long-distance relationship. (Was this deja-vu?) I was not buying these lame excuses and I was starting to get angry.

"What is this *really* about?" I inquired.

"It's too much work" was her reply.

"What is *your* suggestion? I give you option after option which you don't like, so what do *you* have to contribute?" I asked angrily.

"I have no suggestion, because there is no solution" she replied.

"So… just so I understand, you are saying that this relationship isn't worth the work to fix? So that's it?" I pressed.

After a pause she stated "Yes, that is correct." I was practically reeling from the shock of what I had just heard. A myriad of emotions was welling up inside of me ranging from disbelief to rage. Wasn't she the one that called me two days ago with her relationship epiphany? Wasn't she the one that had said *just last night* that she wanted this relationship to work?

"I just don't think this situation is right."

"I just don't think YOU are right…in the head!" I angrily replied. "Do me a favor," I began very slowly and carefully, "do not contact me anymore in any fashion, ever again."

"I won't" she responded quietly.

"I no longer have the patience for you!" Those were my last words as I hung up.

Phone calls immediately launched to Tara and Amy. They were surprised, but at the same time, not so surprised.

I entered the kitchen and as my mother entered the room, and I relayed to her what had just transpired. She was almost as shocked as I was. In an instance of acute emotional trauma, two women are very likely to have a nonsensical, cyclical exchange which may sound something like this:

"Can you believe this??"

"I don't believe it."

"No, I mean, can you really, *actually* believe that??"

"No, I think it is absolutely unbelievable!"

"It is *completely* unbelievable!"

Very soon afterwards, my cousin Jake entered the house and was immediately updated on my relationship situation. Jake has the makings of a stand-up comedian as he is quite entertaining; he is over at the house so often, he could very well be mistaken for a fixture. In the midst of drama like this though, I really believe who walked into the house at that moment was irrelevant, because regardless of who they were, they were *going to be* updated on my relationship situation. Dare I say, even an unsuspecting burglar breaking into the house at that very moment would not have been granted immunity: "You want the TV? No problem! Why don't you sit down a minute and have some coffee, because boy have I got a story for you!"

My mother and my cousin now began to formulate a theory amongst themselves that undoubtedly Shari's mother had something to do with this abrupt turn-around in Shari's behavior.

Jake said that he'd like to bet me fifty dollars (that he admitted he didn't have, and this is why he would have "liked to") that I would be hearing from Shari again before 3 p.m. tomorrow, despite my explicit instructions not to contact me. I figuratively bet that he was wrong (and I say figuratively because truthfully, I didn't have the spare fifty bucks either!) She would not be contacting me. Why would she? She was free and clear now, and she (and her mother) could now both breathe a sigh of relief.

It wasn't quite an hour and I received a text message from Shari. It said "I feel like a total jerk- I am so sorry." Although admittedly a barrage of crude replies came to mind, I had no intention of responding; I was too busy preparing for a funeral.

It appeared our relationship has just died.

Day Twelve: Dream Interpretation Part II

Justin Timberlake tells me not to worry about it, and reminds me that "What Goes Around" will indeed come back around...

Last night I had a dream that I was dating a former cheerleader. I could not readily identify this woman as someone I had known in actual life (although truth be told, she was pretty hot, in a somewhat bitchy-dirty-blond-Britney-Spears kind of way.) In the dream we were at what appeared to be a class reunion and she was getting upset by the lack of acknowledgement she was experiencing due to having been a captain of the cheerleading squad. She was even going to lengths to demonstrate that she still knew certain routines. Some guests at the party watched uncomfortably as they stood around in silence, and it was somewhat awkward. We left the party and were heading towards the parking lot; she was visibly upset. She stopped me and turned me towards her. She looked me in the eyes and asked me in complete seriousness if I was going to be "the one", the girlfriend she always dreamed about. I told her that I was that one (although admittedly without any real passion or conviction) and she was happy. We got in my car to leave and the dream ended.

The first aspect of this dream that immediately stood out to me was that I was dating a *cheerleader*. I had referenced myself as a cheerleader throughout my relationship with Shari, because I was the one who was at times disgustingly optimistic about our situation. It is safe to say that I have a healthy level of vanity, so it makes me laugh that I would portray myself as this attractive, snobby girl from high school. So my "representative", the cheerleader, is desperately going through the motions to prove that she is not washed-up, and that her skill still does amount to something. Meanwhile everyone else around her sees the pathetic display for what it really is and in essence is saying, "Give it up already." Ouch! Okay Subconscious, point taken!

The walk back to my car in my dream, and the confrontation I experienced in the parking lot, may be interpreted on a slightly broader scale. In real life, this was the kind of conversation Shari and I would have frequently. She confessed to me that she had never truly loved anyone the way that she had loved me, and it scared her. I was what she termed her "Big Love". She was prone to crying episodes because she would become so emotional over the perceived depth of our relationship. (This actually concerned me to an extent, but she would assure me that these frequent tearful displays brought on by overwhelming feelings were a *good* thing.) We actually started reading books on Tantric practices together, so we could appreciate our connection on an entirely deeper level. Given our intimate background, it just makes yesterday's outcome all the more surreal. It feels like the "Big Love" was a "Big Lie." As far as my infamous "list" goes (the one that I made earlier in the week to aid in my recovery) I don't think I'll be needing it now after all.

This morning I received a call from my friend, Jared, who wanted to know if I cared to join him for breakfast. I certainly obliged him although I was not fond of his choice in dining establishment. We have a rule though: the inviter pays the bill, and the invitee must endure the location of the proposed breakfast.

Jared is a unique individual, to say the least. We met when I had owned my previous business, a doggy daycare and kennel, and he came to board his dog, Rusty, for the day. Rusty is a psychotic, unsocialized German Shepherd that did *not* end up staying at my facility. The funny part is that Jared strikes the general public as a psychotic, unsocialized individual himself and he is a self-proclaimed sociopath. He makes feeble attempts to date women approximately twice a year, but doesn't seem to understand that not many females are drawn to men who very much resemble the F.B.I. profile of the notorious Unabomber. Ironically, he is a state trooper.

We met at the restaurant and once seated embarked upon an always entertaining exchange. He likes to compare us to Jerry and Elaine from *Seinfeld*, which isn't completely inaccurate. Today he commented that we really do need a George and a Kramer to complete the scenario, to which I agreed.

He inquired as to how my manuscript for the book was coming, which he playfully renames with each inquiry. Today it was: *My Journal of 28 Crazy Lesbians on the Radio*. He then did his best Homer Simpson impersonation as he said lustily, "28 crazy lesbians…" I was trying to ascertain at that moment exactly why I took him up on this breakfast offer.

Jared was anxious to share some news with me, and I could tell by his unordinary level of enthusiasm and chipper demeanor. When I asked him who or what was responsible for this distinct change in biorhythm, he replied only by placing a magazine on the table and pushing it towards me; the cover of it read *Vision*. It was a catalog of organizations recruiting individuals interested in pursuing religious vocations.

Jared then announced that he was considering joining the "Monkhood."

I was more surprised at the fact that I was surprised by his declaration.

In reality, the man was practically a monk already, just without the snazzy wardrobe. He enjoyed being a loner and looked forward to a life of religious contemplation and restful solitude. "Besides," he added, "love and romance are completely overrated" as if his justification would have made his opinion more palatable to me. As I flipped through the magazine, I found myself drawn to some of the ads for various convents. Right about now, that didn't sound like that bad of a lifestyle change, actually. I eventually voiced that I would support any path he chose, but had to throw in for what it was worth, that I would appreciate him at least choosing a Brotherhood that would allow us to still go out to breakfast on occasion; he laughed and assured me that he would look into it.

Throughout breakfast we discussed the other usual topics including family, and work-related issues. We touched upon news and movies. Our best conversation though was reserved for the topic of relationships. Jared was married once, and does not like to admit to it. His marriage lasted approximately three months.

I got him up to speed on the drama that *was* my relationship, and he listened, finding my account of yesterday genuinely entertaining. The thing I enjoy most about conversing with Jared is he has the ability to have very deep and analytical discussions that really get to the root of an argument. (Shari was once witness to one of our five minute debates concerning the topic of pancakes; she later confessed that she found the whole exchange quite maddening.) He believes that some relationships are indeed too much work and that they warrant abandonment. (Imagine that, a sociopath, in favor of abandoning a relationship!) I posed the argument that all couples are capable of making this claim, and if everyone subscribed to this opinion, then we would have no long-term, monogamous couples that we could refer to in order to establish a standard! In typical Jared fashion he claimed that he has not done the adequate research required to prove or refute my theory, but that this needed to be done. I did not foresee Jared interviewing long-term couples to solicit their opinion on the matter, so we could just consider this argument a draw and left the restaurant shortly thereafter.

I called Amy on my way home from breakfast and she was in the process of driving to Rachel's house to spend the weekend. So far Rachel's mother has kept her word and was not giving Rachel anymore grief about her current relationship. I was not entirely convinced that they have heard the last of that mamma-drama, though. I was sensing some piranhas lurking in the waters…

The irony in all of this is that Amy used to tell me that it would bother her when I would go to stay with Shari for a week or two at a time because she would start to miss me. Even though Amy and I don't see each other very often, we do speak several times a day.

Amy is only going to be gone for the weekend, but I now knew exactly how she felt.

Day Thirteen: Productivity

Jo Dee Messina is absolutely right! I've got better things to do than sit around and mope, so "Bye Bye" Lover!

I am happy to say that today I was particularly productive. Most people might normally consider Sunday a "day of rest", but this was not the case for me. I took advantage of the excess free time to get some projects done which I had been putting off.

Also within the realm of "staying busy" is the interesting correlation between recent breakups and trips to the gym. I have resurrected my health club membership as of late. I think the gym provides the perfect combination of purpose, stress relief, and an excuse to work on our vanity (seeing as we are now technically "back on the market".) Private revelation: I don't foresee dating again for a *long* time.

I thought about Shari intermittently today.

I vacillated between missing her and damning her to Hell.

It is unfortunate when anger factors into your breakup, but this was undoubtedly what has given me the strength to distance myself from the situation, although for that I am grateful. I would actually rather feel angry than sad, and had we left well enough alone in the beginning and never attempted to reconcile, I would undoubtedly be venturing towards a significant depression at this moment.

I did wonder how she was getting along. I wondered if she regretted her decision at all. Sometimes we regret a particular breakup. During the course of various relationships, a certain person may come along once (or maybe even twice) in a lifetime and leave a lasting impression on us for years to come. When that relationship dissipates, the residual effects may be more potent than originally anticipated. Although "regret" is not regarded as a healthy emotion, at the very least, you may find yourself *wondering* about decisions you may have made at the time regarding your relationship. I think Wonder is in the same family tree as Curiosity, and therefore quite natural. So you may ask yourself a variety of questions which are preceded by "what if" and continue to visualize a completely hypothetical future with your former partner, had circumstances been different.

As for me, the only regret I am experiencing at the moment is the fact that we didn't stay broken up last summer.

Day Fourteen: What the Radio Said

If we are all "So Sick" of nauseating love songs, why can't we turn off our radios? Good question, Ne-Yo.

It's hard to believe that all of this was set into motion two weeks ago today! On one hand it feels like much longer, when realistically we only "officially" broke up (again) three days ago. (Wait a minute- did we ever officially reconcile?!) According to my calculations, it has been nearly two and a half weeks since we've *physically* seen each other, and I think it's this kind of long-distance arrangement which is making it easier to get over. I could be wrong, though. I am certain that there are those that would dispute this claim of mine by saying if I were really in love to the degree that I had stated, then I would not be as composed as I am now. Perhaps that is true. Perhaps subconsciously I *knew* that we weren't capable of seeing this relationship through; perhaps having the dreams about dating other women was a hint!

I spent a good deal of time in my car today and therefore spent the majority of my time listening to the radio. I heard an interesting ensemble of songs today, all of which I could apply to my current relationship situation.

"Goodbye to You" from Scandal made an entertaining debut on my radio. It's your run-of-the-mill, general break up song, served up with a dash of "Good riddance!" I felt I could certainly extract a line or two and apply them to my ego where needed. Next up, was "Far Away" from Nickelback. When Shari and I broke up over the summer for our six-week interval, this song had some particular significance. This is a perfect song for couples involved in long-distance relationships that have broken up and are content to dwell upon that fact. Happily for me, the effects of this particular song have somewhat waned. The last song by Pink entitled "Who Knew" might have had more sting to it, had I the opportunity to listen to it in its entirety. (My thanks to whichever deity was responsible for the cosmic intervention which spared me anymore than I had been subjected to!) This catchy number really does a good job of summarizing my surprise and disappointment by the entire chain of events in our relationship (all subconscious notifications aside.)

I have a special place in my heart for the song "Believe" by Cher. When I am feeling particularly brassy I like to contribute my robust vocal backup to this technologically-enhanced anthem of resilience. What I wouldn't give for the opportunity to sit around with Cher one afternoon sipping tea and absorbing some of her wisdom and fabulousness as if through osmosis; oh, the stories I bet she could tell! The song begs the question: is there life after love? That is the burning question after all, isn't it?

I spoke with Karen today. She was flying back home from San Francisco today. Being the good (and occasionally self-absorbed) friend that I am, I completely forgot that Karen was going to California this weekend. I instantly remembered though that prior to her breakup with Angel, the original plan was for them to go California together to take advantage of a friend's timeshare in San Francisco. I couldn't *not* ask what happened between them over the weekend! Karen told me that they got along famously, and that they had a mutually sad parting. As I listened to this, I was reading something into her story which forced me to ask: "So what does this mean?" I dreaded the response. The answer was that Karen was giving Angel another chance. (Taking another chance with the hot stove, eh?) I inquired as to what happened with catching Angel on the online dating site seeking men. Karen said it was a setup: Angel created that profile as "a test" to see if Karen would check up on her, and she clearly failed. I thought to myself "Does she really believe what she is saying to me at this moment?" That is not the real issue at hand anyway. The *real* issue is that Karen has a problem with the fact that Angel lives with her "ex" girlfriend. Karen has always been suspicious of their allegedly platonic relationship which makes me wonder if transgendered individuals are capable of having "women's intuition." Regardless, I do believe that all human beings are endowed with instinct, and this was Karen's screaming at her. This woman Angel was just bad news, period.

I couldn't listen to this anymore and told Karen as much. I told her she didn't need this. She shared with me the trials and tribulations of being transgendered, and stated that she would never find anyone as remotely attractive as Angel to date; Karen also suffers from low self-esteem, which just perpetuates the cycle. I personally cannot fathom how hard it must be to try to enter the dating realm as transgendered, but I believe I can empathize to an extent. The irony is that our own gay and lesbian community can be so hypocritical and judgmental towards these individuals as well. Hell, dating is hard enough! Imagine if you've physiologically changed your entire identity! I threateningly told her that if she didn't stop all of this pessimism at once, I was going to go on a date with her just for the sake of proving her wrong! She responded by telling me she didn't want a "pity date" and besides, she claimed she was too headstrong for me anyway. I laughed because I knew she was right.

Towards evening, I had finally caught up with Amy who has relayed to me that there was much drama and commotion over the weekend at Rachel's house. (I'm hardly surprised.) It appeared that Rachel had some relatives unexpectedly stop by to visit, and conveniently as Amy was getting out of the shower! They managed to fake their way through an entirely awkward situation, long enough to appease their visitors. Later in the day though, phone calls fired around Rachel's family tree, revelations were made, tears were shed, and all was in disarray. Luckily somehow, some of the dust had settled by nightfall and things appeared as though they might be alright after all; the rest of the family was just adjusting to the news. I give Amy a lot of credit for sticking with Rachel during all of this, because obviously it is a very stressful time in their relationship. I think if they can make it through these trials though, then the rest of the relationship will be a piece of cake.

I'm proud of them: they are dealing with their piranhas, and that's the way it should be.

Day Fifteen: Cheerleading Dangers

Nobody is "Irreplaceable", Baby...Nobody.

I saw online today an article discussing the topic of cheerleading dangers; I found that slightly amusing. Not that I think that the possibility of these adolescent girls getting seriously injured is humorous, but the fact that I equated the title of this article with something completely unrelated (or more aptly, relationship related) made me laugh to myself.

Yes, we can draw a distinct parallel here: in a relationship context there is a danger to your heart and ego in cheerleading when no one wants or seemingly appreciates your support. After all, you'd feel kind of silly if you were, in actuality, part of a squad and you were the only one cheering. You would undoubtedly grow a little tired of being the only one displaying robust enthusiasm. You might even consider changing squads, and go where others shared your passion for cheering, as you should.

I have felt lately that a kind of weight has been lifted off of me. I don't know how to phrase it exactly, but I have felt small surges of motivation and optimism as far as my future is concerned. I am enjoying becoming acquainted with my new found contentment.

Today was a day for more reflection on events past. I spoke with Amy today about relationships and our philosophies surrounding them. I realize that we as human beings don't always possess the ability to be objective about the negative role we may play in relationships, so I asked Amy from her perspective, what my contribution to the demise of this relationship may have been. I knew Amy would answer me truthfully, even if it wasn't what I wanted to hear. She answered that although she could see how at times I could be considered somewhat demanding and high-maintenance, she really could not see how that warranted ending our relationship. She commended me for really trying to work things out and suggesting therapy.

Ever notice that when a couple breaks up, generally each party thinks that they somehow came out ahead? It is a popular and prevalent idea that the end of any relationship is clearly the *other* partner's loss and that the *other* partner most certainly got the short end of the proverbial stick by breaking up with *us*. *We* are so much better off without *them*. They will never find anyone as good as us. What fools they were! I think we do this primarily for ego preservation. People generally have trouble admitting their faults to start, so this is a reasonable reaction, in my mind.

My problem is though that I actually believe this to be the case in my relationship and damn it, I feel justified in my belief!

I provided endless examination of the relationship during its existence and I was the one who made the majority of the efforts to preserve it! Now, by this admission I realize I run the risk of sounding like a martyr (or a fool... I think there is a fine line between the two.) Well, so be it! Just add it to the list: I am a demanding, high-maintenance, overly-analytical fool of a martyr!

She'll never do better.

Day Sixteen: Oh How Time Flies

The song "Always Something There to Remind Me" just
reminded me of all the cursed reminders of her!

I made an accidental discovery today when I looked at my calendar. I noticed some notes scratched out on three specific days, the first of which being tomorrow. The event that had been scratched out was the one year anniversary of my first email to Shari.

Females are fond of memorializing dates and events. As a matter of fact, in this particular relationship, Shari and I had *three* different anniversary dates. There was the first time I emailed her, the first time we spoke on the phone, and the first time we actually met. All three of these events took place within a two week window, so this should be an interesting next couple of days! Believe it or not, I was terrible at remembering these anniversaries. Don't ask me why, but truth be told, that was part of the reason I wrote them on the calendar; I didn't want to be caught off guard the day of the big event! Normally I am very good about remembering such things, so I'm not sure if I should read anything into my apparent lack of attention to detail in this particular relationship.

There is also the act of collecting affectionate tokens as well. You may have a shoebox or perhaps a special drawer which holds little artifacts from excursions you have had with your significant other.

You may have tangible evidence of a memorable outing, and you long to preserve it, because even though average movie ticket stubs don't normally make you feel warm and fuzzy, these particular ones do.

I have heard that the strongest memory stimulator in humans is smell. Shari and I went through a phase because we didn't see each other that often, I would leave her with a piece of my clothing (that had preferably been worn by me prior, per her request) and amply saturated in my perfume. She would reciprocate the gesture as well which I found to be very endearing, and I believe she did as well (until the day she attempted to sleep with one of my fragrant shirts and woke up with a migraine!)

I would be lying if I said I wasn't curious to see if Shari attempts to contact me on any one of these three days. I sadly laugh to myself and think at certain points during this relationship things were going *so* well, I really didn't foresee this split *ever* coming. And now, tomorrow would be one year since I contacted Shari online, the same woman that I considered committing the rest of my life to, and now we are not even speaking.

Pink said it best in her song: "Who knew?"

Day Seventeen: Dream Interpretation Part III

I think Meredith Brooks knew she had a potential PMS anthem on her hands when she wrote the song, "Bitch".

I had a dream last night that I was in an airport and had just arrived back into Chicago, from what I'm presuming was Atlanta (but I'm not sure because the entire flight portion was deleted.) I was leaving the airport, walking with droves of people towards the exit. Next thing I know, I am walking alone on a large sidewalk along what looks like the ocean. The ground and the short, winding wall to my right which follows the curve of the path are almost blindingly white. Is this California? I am alone, but I am not lonely and there is a contentment I am experiencing. I am marveling at the water to my left which is a beautiful blue, and for that matter, so is the sky on this perfect, sunny, cloudless day! For an instant in the dream, I wondered what Shari was doing, and if it was as nice out where she was, and then the dream ended.

I actually liked my dream, and interpret it as: things are good, and they are just going to get better. Even though I may have been mildly stressed yesterday about the anticipation of my upcoming anniversaries, I am happy to report that I woke up feeling pretty good!

As the day wore on, however …

I grew suspicious that I may have been tiptoeing into the realm of PMS. I began to feel a tad moody and I'm also sick to death of hearing the song "It's not over" by Daughtry. I was ready to yell back, "IT SURE IS, SO GET OVER IT ALREADY!"

I spoke to Tara last night and she filled me in on her wonderful getaway. Tara and Lori had a good time, but had a few rough patches once they got home (and I was left with the impression that Lori's ex-girlfriend was one of those patches.) Lori is quite *gradually* transitioning out of her former relationship, and testing Tara's patience along the way.

Amy and Rachel are doing well. As a matter of fact, they have yet to have a real "fight". They did have a good tiff once though and "tiffing", as all women are well aware of, is the prelude to "fighting". This was the kind of tiff where Rachel threatened to leave Amy's place because of a petty misunderstanding. What made me laugh was hearing Amy's account of the story, and how disturbed she was because her apartment was too small for them to escape one another while the tiff was occurring! I know that feeling all too well: you don't even want to be in the same room with one another! God forbid a fight should occur in the evening, and you don't resolve things. What happens when it comes time to go to bed then? Which one of you is sleeping on the couch?

I was a tad surprised that I didn't hear from Shari at all today. On top of it being one of our anniversaries, it was also Shari's day off. I wonder if she spends as much time thinking about our situation as I do. I would love to be a fly on the wall at her place! All in all, I'm not that upset that she didn't call …

There really wouldn't have been anything to say anyway.

Day Eighteen: Dream Interpretation Part IV

It is so sad, because it slowly is becoming
"Like We Never Loved At All."

Last night I had a disturbing dream that I lost a tooth! I was looking in a mirror and I could see that one of my front bottom teeth was very loose, and I simply plucked it out. When I looked down into my gums, I could see the remnant of a black root. That sufficiently grossed me out (not to mention, threw me into a small panic because now I was missing a very visible tooth!)

I mentioned the dream to Amy later in the morning, who had the following comfort to share:

"I think losing a tooth in a dream means that you're going to die."

"Oh great! Thanks a lot! Why would you tell me that? Even if you think it is true, you could have lied!" I responded in quite a tizzy.

"I'm sorry!" Amy offered, having realized her error. "I'm not sure. Ask Karen. I'm sure she'd know what it means."

Shortly thereafter we conclude our telephone conversation. Within minutes, Karen is calling me.

"Speak of the Diablo!" I exclaimed. "Amy and I were just speaking about you!" I then explained to her my distress about having had a toothless dream, to which she promptly reassured me that it had nothing to do with death (in the sense that one might interpret it, anyway.)

Karen's take on my dream is that it is representative of my "dead" relationship with Shari. Here is an interesting detail which I hadn't previously considered prior to my conversation with Karen: there was absolutely no pain when I excised the tooth. I'm intrigued. Karen told me that she believes that this relationship may truthfully be over, black root and all. I may have to agree.

Today was Good Friday, and this should have been the day that I drove down to Atlanta to housesit while Shari went to Florida to spend Easter with her family. The thought of Boomer being boarded at the vet's office really doesn't sit well with me, but unfortunately there is nothing I can do about it. Funny, I think *that* upsets me more than anything else about this weekend! I know that Shari is going to drive down to Florida one-way with her mother tonight, and it's about a ten hour drive. I wonder if I will come up in conversation. Shari had expressed to me in the past how her patience would wane after being together with her mother for a certain amount of time (particularly during lengthy car rides) together. I believe on significant road trips everyone can become a little irritable with their traveling companions; the key is enjoying the road trip itself in the first place. (I personally love road trips; Shari hates them.)

Karen surprised me by calling me late in the evening. She was audibly upset and needed to talk, so I most certainly made myself available. She said that she had spoken to Angel earlier in the evening and told the woman never to contact her again. Karen was fed up with ignoring her own instincts and being played for a fool. I listened sympathetically, but doubted the sincerity of this maneuver, after all, *that stove is just so tempting!*

By the time our conversation drew to an end, Karen said she felt somewhat better after speaking with me. I'm just glad I could be of assistance. Sure, men have their "bonding" rituals, but women have moments of genuine "sisterhood" where we really do have a deeper level of understanding of one another's plights and emotions. I really think that's why lesbianism really isn't all that big of a jump for many women, because emotionally, we're halfway there already! I think it troubles some women to really explore who their most emotionally intimate connections are with, the answers can be surprising.

I'm still discovering a few surprises myself.

Day Nineteen: Tired

"What's Love Got to Do with It?" Everything.

I woke up incredibly and inexplicably tired today. I don't really know what to attribute it to, but it could be any variety of things. I think I will blame it on a lack of vitamins (which reminds me, I forgot to take my vitamins today.)

I spoke with my mom today about my former relationship. My mother shared with me her thought that if Shari wasn't regretting her decision to break up by now, she probably soon would be. She also predicted that Shari would probably be acutely aware when she returned from her Easter weekend, that the dogs and I should have been at the house waiting. I do wonder.

I had intermittent thoughts of Shari today, but I am keeping myself busy, you know! Occasionally a sweet, unanticipated thought slipped in there under the radar. I did look at a few pictures of her today, and I'm having mixed emotions. I recognized the person in the picture as someone I had loved intensely, but the feelings are beginning to change already. (Sure, I say this now, but if we were come face to face I'm not entirely sure I wouldn't be reduced to a blubbering mess!)

I have a few things at Shari's that I had requested to be returned to me. I was speaking with Amy about the topic, and trying to determine if Shari's delay is due to emotional attachment or simple procrastination.

Shari is a textbook procrastinator (which was another tell-tale sign of our impending relationship doom.) For God's sake, she didn't dispose of her X-mas tree until the middle of March! Amy thinks its simple procrastination; I think maybe it's a combination of both (but then again maybe I flatter myself!)

Amy and Rachel make me laugh. Watching them in the infancy stage of their relationship makes me realize how disgusting new love really is for outsiders (especially single outsiders!) They see each other faithfully every weekend, and this weekend they weren't supposed to see one another due to the holiday. (I knew that arrangement wouldn't last, for they are together!) I tease Amy and tell her that she and Rachel couldn't do what Shari and I did; they wouldn't make it seeing each other every two to three weeks! That's hardcore, right there! Amy agreed wholeheartedly.

I still do on occasion check my email and phone for text messages, although it seems silly. I read something in the news today which related to a story that Shari and I had discussed in the past, and naturally she was the first one that I thought of calling … I told her never to contact me again and she agreed. The last time we broke up, she was the one to break the ice with a text message.

I wonder if this time she will keep her end of the bargain.

Day Twenty: Restless Night

*No ... The emotions are still too raw and
"I'm not ready to make nice."*

I had a horrible night's sleep last night! My mind was racing non-stop throughout the night! I was overloaded with work thoughts, and that rarely happens. I remember dreaming frequently off and on, but I can't recall anything specifically. I'm sure Shari was in the montage though; it amazes me at how often I dream about her, both now and throughout the course of our relationship. It's crazy! I don't feel so badly though: Shari has said the same exact thing about marveling at her frequency of dreams of me.

Today was Easter. I'm thankful that my family wasn't planning on having a houseful of guests, and that my role as cook was extremely limited. Overall, it had been a pretty lazy Sunday.

My stepfather asked me today if I had heard from Shari at all. I was actually surprised that he asked (or was I just surprised that someone mentioned her name?) I said that I had not heard from her. I have been tempted once or twice to call her, because I do not like the way that we left things. I was evidently angry, and I believe I conveyed that message rather effectively, but when I think about it though, I still am angry, and don't think it would be wise to try to have a casual conversation at this point.

I know that she is coming back home tonight after her holiday weekend with her family. She will be arriving home to an empty house. That would disturb me, personally, but I wonder if it will bother her. Actually I can guess that it will bother her, but I suppose I just question to what degree. I mean, even Boomer will still be boarding at the vet! There is nothing like the feeling of walking into a very large house when it is devoid of any other living activity; it's rather lonely I think.

It's amazing all the things you can get accomplished when you are single, versus when you are in a relationship. You have all kinds of time, and much less distraction. You're productive, you go to the gym more regularly, you see more of your friends; this single thing really isn't all that bad! Once you get used to the feeling of a seeping hole in the center of your chest where your heart used to be, it's practically all downhill!

Luckily, I have been able to fend off the majority of those intimate, warm and fuzzy memories. I will say though, that so far every time I pass the floral section at the grocery store, without fail, I think about bringing Shari flowers. For the longest time, whenever I drove down to see her, I would bring some simple arrangement of flowers. Once, I was tempted to pull over on the highway to pick her some beautiful lavender wildflowers which were growing with reckless abandon. I didn't though, and it was probably because I was too intent on reaching my destination as quickly as possible (or I was afraid of being demolished by a careening tractor trailer barreling down the interstate.) I think flowers picked by hand have more a more raw sentimental potency, versus your run-of-the-mill commercial arrangement. In retrospect, I'm very sorry I never brought her the wildflowers …

It brings a whole new meaning to the term "sweet nothings", eh?

Day Twenty-One: Swingin' Moods

Are women really the fickle lunatics Billy Joel makes us out to be in "She's Always A Woman"?

One of the glorious aspects of being a woman is the hormonally-induced mood swings we experience at least a few days out of every month. I know I have been somewhat touchy as of late, but Amy has told me it is very evident by the irritable tones of my emails.

I found myself having a sentimental moment today while I was out running errands; my mind was just drifting around throughout various memories. That all came to a screeching halt as a particular song, "Golddigger", came on the radio.

About two months ago, I had joked with Shari while standing in her kitchen by saying that it was evident that the only reason she was staying with me was because she knew my website was going to be a huge success and I was going to eventually become a millionaire. Believe it or not, she took offense to this, because it was not the first time I had made this joke, and she feared that I might believe this was true of her. I proceeded to sing a few lines from the Kanye West song "Golddigger" and referenced the part that states that the woman in the song is not wasting her time with any broke man. To that Shari responded, "I'm not?" She thought that was very funny and a fine time to take advantage of a perfect joke set-up. I, on the other, hand felt like all the wind had just been knocked out of me, but in Shari's eyes I was just being "too sensitive."

I inserted myself into a *Dream On* moment of a clip from one of my all-time favorite movies, *Taxi Driver*. De Niro would have been proud of my performance, as part of me was privately discerning, "Is she talking *to me?* She must be talking to me. I don't see anyone else here!"

My situation is admittedly a touchy one. It is very difficult at times to have experienced a major financial setback, maintain a positive attitude and stay motivated to press forward. The last thing anyone in this situation needs is to be reminded of that failure. I never in a million years would have expected that kind of insensitivity from my lover. The band Everlast wrote a song with a similar sentiment which declares that before we judge anyone or their situation, we should all take a walk in someone else's shoes for a day; it's a great lesson in humility.

As the day went on, I reflected on what I had written of the previous days; I was really fixed on figuring out why I had said that I didn't think I was capable of speaking with Shari yet because I was *angry*. As a rule I do not get angry, and if I do, it is fleeting, at best. What was I angry about? I continued to ponder.

Initially I believed I was angry with Shari because she dropped this bomb of a breakup on me out of left field. I never saw it coming…

Or did I?

After a second I thought, *I did know this all along.* I knew how she felt about therapy, she had commented numerous times about feeling like we were "too much work" and I absolutely knew how protective and defensive she was of her mother.

HELLO, EINSTEIN? How could any of this have surprised me??

I think she knew since last summer that this breakup was what she wanted, but I raised enough good arguments to cause "reasonable doubt" about our original decision and so we gave it another go (which then summoned the relationship piranhas.) I did not appreciate the emotional rollercoaster throughout the two days leading up to our final breakup and I could be somewhat angry about the fact that THE DAY BEFORE our actual breakup, things seemed really hopeful (and by Shari's account, things were "really going to work out.") I think more than anything, I am angry and disappointed with *myself.* I am notorious for warning people to watch out for "red flags" in relationships, and meanwhile I had a bunch slapping me in the face myself! I'm by no means saying I am entirely blameless, but right now my biggest regret is having held on to the relationship for too long. In my defense though, I think most couples are too quick to give up and throw their banged-up relationships away; I am a fixer and I am a problem solver and damn it, if anyone can make it work, *I can*! I am the "Rosie the Riveter" of lesbian relationship maintenance, bolding stating my motto: "We can do it!" The only catch here is that in order for that philosophy to matter, your partner needs to feel the same way.

Before I met Shari, I actually wrote out a list of traits that I was looking for in an ideal mate. It was a fairly extensive list, and Shari fit the vast majority of my requirements, but after this experience, I can definitely see how a few of my priorities have changed and some details may have been overlooked. My list will have to be modified, clearly.

I received a call from Tara before I went to bed. She has been wanting me to come over and see her new apartment, so she is using this opportunity to lure me over to her abode. She is pulling out all the stops, and has even offered to cook for me! (Oh, the cookies this woman can bake!) In the process of catching me up on little day to day events in between enticements, she told me that she was tiffing with Lori. While we were speaking, Lori actually called Tara on the other phone, which was ignored and directed into voicemail. Tara then replayed the voicemail message loudly enough for me to hear it. Lori, sounding extremely casual in the message, suggested that if they didn't speak tonight, perhaps they could just speak tomorrow; that was only adding to Tara's agitation.

"I'm not calling her. She can just wait now!" Tara stated.

"Why?" I asked. "Why don't you just call her back?"

"No. I'm tired of being so readily available for her. She can wait."

So even though Tara probably did want to speak with Lori, she was going to punish herself *and* Lori because of pride. I was wondering if men partake in such spiteful acts and was asking myself "why do we do things like this?" I know I have engaged in the same behavior (even recently) but as with many other things, actually seeing someone else behave this way, gave it a whole different perspective.

I was amused by Tara's next suggestion that she and I become platonic "companions" which was an option we discussed years ago when we were still a couple. We realize that we always shared a wonderful relationship dynamic, but just couldn't keep our romantic passion alive; we dissolved into a state of friendship. The idea isn't sounding all that unappealing, actually.

Karen had invited me out to brunch to take place this coming Sunday, to which I in turn, invited Tara and Amy because I figured the more the merrier. Amy had accepted my invitation earlier in the day, so after I received a positive response to my brunch invitation from Tara, we ended our phone conversation and I eagerly went to bed.

Day Twenty-Two: Impulses

"One Way or Another" this is all going to be resolved.

I will blame it on the hormones: I *almost* called Shari today. I had been MISSING HER LIKE CRAZY on and off all throughout the day! I felt like all the feelings about our relationship that I crammed down came boiling to the surface in an instant! This is insane! I read somewhere once that if you can fend of the first ten seconds of an impulsive urge, then you have it beaten. I was actually mildly panicked for a second, and felt like I needed a support group sponsor to call! (Then again, that's exactly why I have Amy, Tara and Karen; aka my brunch-support-therapy group!) I am happy to report that the impulse philosophy is true: I was able to hold out for ten seconds and overcome the temptation to call.

Amy made me laugh today (which is a common occurrence) by sharing something that she had done which was in the same vein as Tara's spiteful act yesterday. She had been trying to figure out her plans with Rachel for this coming weekend, and had not been receiving the adequate input or enthusiasm from her partner.

"Has Rachel given you an answer about this weekend yet?" I asked.

"No," Amy replied, "and I'm not going to bring it up again!"

"Now why would you do that? You want to know! Just ask and get it over with!"

Ugh! The games women play! I then shared with Amy what Tara pulled with Lori the day before, and drew some parallels between their behaviors that inspired some laughter. I dislike coyness myself, and this is exactly how Amy and Rachel are acting. I also dislike brats, and Amy has the ability, on occasion, to be quite the brat. Everyone has the ability to express some discontent in a situation or relationship, but I reserve the term "brat" for someone (most often a woman) who gets extremely short, and spiteful in response to something that doesn't meet with their approval. Amy's patented brat response usually comes out over the phone, when she has been unjustly offended (or joked on) to which she curtly replies: "I have to go!" This statement confirms that a great offense has taken place. Most times there is no use in trying to ascertain what the injustice was, because more often than not if you ask what the problem is at that particular point, you will receive the ever-famous response: "Nothing." The singer Edie Brockell hit in on the head when she said once that there is nothing worse than "nothing".

I don't have the patience for brats but luckily I don't encounter that behavior all that often. Shari could admittedly be quite bratty herself at times...

On one occasion, not all that long ago, Shari had taken me out to dinner during one of my visits. We went to a very nice steakhouse in an upscale suburb of Atlanta, but the mood between us had begun to change: Shari was fairly stiff, and was not comfortable giving any indication that we were a lesbian couple due to our conservative surroundings. Mind you, I wasn't requesting that we make out at the table, but just reciprocate some degree of warmth. After dinner, we had our leftovers wrapped and proceeded home. Once we were back at the house, I decided to give one of my dogs a portion of my steak from the dinner. This did not sit well with Shari *at all.* An argument commenced including both the awkwardness at dinner and MY right to feed MY dog MY leftovers even though it was bought for ME. My mind was working overtime, trying to separate and address both issues.

I will never forget, at one point, while in the process of suggesting a compromise on one of the issues, Shari loudly responded quite angrily "Why do we have to compromise on *everything*! I'm sick of compromising! Why can't some things just BE?" The rest of the night ended horribly, with her threatening to sleep in the guest bedroom. I had never seen her so cold and unrecognizable, and told her so. I made one last attempt to talk to her as she was preparing her sleeping arrangements in the spare bedroom, pleading with her to come to bed. She did end up coming to bed, and the next day apologized for her behavior. She said she couldn't believe she had acted that way towards me and it "broke her heart" that I had to come to her in that delicate manner. She "felt like a big ass." Looking back, I'd say she was right.

I am so glad I didn't call.

Being that my occupation is in the pet industry, I correspond regularly with various pet professionals throughout the city. One of the business owners I speak with on occasion is Andy who is an award-winning dog trainer. We have never spoken outside of a professional context before, although he did jokingly ask me out on a date once (which Shari knew about, and did not care for whatsoever.) I had exchanged emails with Andy today, which led to another date request. I wasn't sure how to handle this situation. I didn't feel comfortable saying "I'm seeing someone" because in the current case, I wasn't, and also I would have felt like a hypocrite hiding my orientation. I shared my dilemma with Amy, who of course found this deliciously amusing. I decided that I was going to call him and tell him the truth concerning the situation. This is where that line "It's not you, it's me" really does apply!

Andy and I ended up playing a bit of phone tag, but eventually did get a chance to speak briefly by the end of the night. He had just gotten off of work and sounded somewhat hurried. He claimed he needed to "decompress" and absolutely sounded like it. He wanted to meet me tomorrow for dinner and a movie, casually, as friends, of course. ("My God", I'm thinking, "how much more of a stereotypical date could this be: dinner and a movie?") He really enjoys foreign films and stated that was what he would like to do. (I thought, if this *was* a date, how about asking the lady what she'd like to do? Guys just don't get it.) I do like foreign films myself, and indicated as much, but before I could say anything more, our evening plans for tomorrow had just been confirmed! We hung up the phone, and I was trying my best to convince myself that I had not just made a "date" with this man.

I called Amy with the update, and she assured me, that I did just that.

Day Twenty-Three: Talking to Pictures

*I know I shouldn't look at these "Pictures of You" for
so long, Shari, but I just can't help myself...*

Amy quit her job today. I sent her a text saying, "Enjoy your last day of work!" She responded by sending me a text that said, "Enjoy your 'boy date' tonight." I still had yet to address that issue, I am reminded. Unless I wanted to be the tormented, outcast lesbian from the movie *Chasing Amy*, I had to address it sooner than later. So I did what any forthcoming, practical woman would do: I sent an email.

Before outing myself to him I explained to Andy that I thought he was a wonderful person by using the "it's not you, it's me" speech. I went on to say that I would love to get together with him for dinner sometime, within the proper context, of course. He responded shortly thereafter, very grateful for my honesty, and said that by all means we should still plan on getting together when it was convenient. Overall, I was pleased with how our encounter had gone.

I was cleaning out my laptop today and found a couple of stray pictures of Shari. In one of the pictures she had attempted to crop out the image of her ex-girlfriend. That picture made me laugh because you can still see the remnant of the ex-girlfriend in the picture, and that was one of the first pictures she ever sent to me when we were courting online, amusingly enough. Hmmmm. Will she crop me out of pictures and use them to court other women? That thought disturbed me slightly.

As I looked at that particular picture, I actually surprised myself by muttering aloud, "Look at those cold, grey eyes." Her eyes are kind of a grey-greenish color, but knowing what I know now, they struck me as particularly cold. Actually, any of my friends or family that had met Shari all coincidentally used the word "cold" to describe her, but it didn't matter one bit to me: what mattered what was I thought of her, and no one else.

The other picture of us was from a happier time during the summer; it was the day when we went to "our" favorite restaurant, followed by "our" favorite bookstore. We both looked good in the picture, I thought. As I studied that image, I said to myself, "Baby, what did you do?" At times like this it astounded me that she was willing and able to throw our relationship away.

I spoke to Amy today about some memorable, Shari, Jeckyll-and-Hyde moments. Shari had a hair-trigger when it came to getting emotional about *some* things, but not things that would generally move the masses. Things that moved me to tears such as September 11th, Princess Diana's funeral, or maybe even a particularly touching episode of *ER* didn't faze her. She would however cry quite readily and somewhat frequently as a result of being "overwhelmed" by her feelings of love for me (how ironic.) Amy delicately referenced her past prediction that it was evident from the start that my relationship with Shari was at a disadvantage due to our differences in organizational habits (Amy is quite a neat freak like me.)

I called Amy once from Shari's house in a mild state of horror and described to her the side of the refrigerator that looked like a bunch of scrap papers and business cards had just exploded and stuck themselves on the appliance randomly wherever they landed. There were dozens of pictures, phone numbers and receipts every which way, creating some kind of informative collage on the refrigerator. I took it upon myself to give the collage a little more order by at least lining things up (and putting them right-side up.) When Shari got home from work she wasn't very happy and said it all looked "too linear" (and apparently her style is more abstract.) The mismatched pattern was rightfully restored soon thereafter. Organization is absolutely going on my "Top 5" desirable traits in a mate next time! What is really funny about this is that Amy used these instances in my relationship as reference points when she and Rachel were courting! She actually asked Rachel what her closets and drawers looked like before they had ever physically met (looking back, I wish I had done the same thing!)

Amy and I came to a conclusion about organized and disorganized people which is this: disorganized people will organize themselves for their mate's sake, but it will never be *important* to them. This poses a problem to those of us that value organization because it really is a fundamental difference that puts us on opposite ends of the spectrum on so many levels. As superficial as it may sound, I want to be with someone who *likes* to be organized because they like to live that way, not simply because it's what I want. When I heard that Hillary Clinton likes to organize closets for fun, that facet alone practically ensured her my vote for President!

There was a word that I would use on occasion that would drive Shari insane, which was "standards." (I actually used it quite regularly until I learned of Shari's abhorrence of the word.) The word "standards" is completely applicable when discussing your expectations of all facets of your life and is reflective, I feel, of your values. I think the fact that Shari had such a strong objection to this word was yet another example of me getting one of those cracks in the face by a red flag.

Day Twenty-Four:
Funny Creatures We Women Are

Oh, Avril, you are SO right on! I could do so much better!

I spoke with Amy on the phone today and we had an interesting discussion regarding phone etiquette. She had called Rachel, and Rachel said she was on the other line and asked if she could call Amy back. Rachel said that was no problem, and they ended their brief conversation.

"Who was she talking to?" I asked, rather surprised that Amy had been let go.

"I don't know" replied Amy.

"How do you not know?" I questioned.

"I didn't ask" came the response.

I felt that had we been having this discussion at this particular juncture in person, I wouldn't have been able to restrain my expression of studious curiosity, similar to that of examining a new insect I had temporarily restrained in a glass before releasing it back into the wild. It would have been very similar to the look she received from me when she first revealed to me that during her post-shower body lotioning, she deliberately lotions her armpits, as well...

I found this interesting because it has been my experience when speaking on the phone with my girlfriends, if another call should necessitate us ending our phone call prematurely, the girlfriend usually divulged the identity of the interrupting caller automatically. For example, if I called at an inopportune moment, Shari would say "Hi Baby, I'm finishing up with so-and-so, can I call you right back?" The vast majority of the time though, that *other* party was dismissed immediately to clear the way for, or to continue the important call from the girlfriend. It's simply "Maslow's Hierarchy of Telephone Priority" (which was later renamed in broader terms as "Maslow's Hierarchy of Needs".) If the identity of the other caller was not divulged in the initial answering of the phone, you could be sure that the question, "Baby, who were you talking to?" was soon to come. We don't call it suspicious, we call it curious.

Who is trumping the high priority girlfriend call? I felt I was actually getting defensive for Amy (probably because I know what happens on our end if we are talking and Rachel calls: Amy can't hang up with me quickly enough! Admittedly, I was the same way with her when Shari called me, though.)

Amy tried to convince me that it is not a matter of importance, but rather a matter of priority. "Who called first" is the rule she claimed to adhere to most times. She is full of crap. (I think too that if I referenced the above example, she would see I have blown a hole in her case!) Amy then went on to affix me (and my girlfriends) with some "controlling" label. I didn't fully agree with that either (based on this criteria, anyway.)

Awhile later I was speaking with Tara on the phone and referenced the incident with Amy. I asked Tara the following question:

"If you called Lori, and she was on the other line and asked if she could call you back without stating who she was speaking with, what would you think?"

"I would say to myself 'Who is that bitch talkin' to?'" Tara admitted. "But I don't know if I would say that out loud, at least not to Lori. You don't want to look all possessive, but I would definitely be thinking it."

I laughed, and started to wonder why Tara and I ever broke up in the first place.

I had a hair appointment at the salon, Pazzo, mid-day which gave me a chance to catch up with my friend and stylist, Deidre. Pazzo is one of the South suburb's best kept secrets when it comes to full service salons; it is staffed with appropriately beautiful people whose job it is to make the rest of us just as beautiful. I was near the reception desk running my hand along the stone inlay of the walls, and appreciating the contrasts between the smooth and rough textures surrounding me, when Diedre came up to greet me.

Diedre can best be described as "scattered", which is a term she does not find offensive. She is constantly on the go but in typical Libra fashion, attempts to incorporate as much fun and zest into her life as possible. Diedre would also be the perfect recipient for the T-shirt that read "Straight, but not narrow" (provided it didn't clash with her particular style that day.) I knew this was going to be an interesting afternoon, because last she knew, Shari and I were the epitome of relationship bliss. I was thinking, "Girl, pull up a chair, 'cause we gotta TALK!"

In between my hair highlights and after preliminary catching up she asked how Shari was, to which I responded, "We broke up." She was stunned, and naturally wanted to know all of the juicy details. I would say doing some emotional venting at a chic, cappuccino-equipped hair salon surrounded by other sympathetic women (and plenty of gay men) does lend a cathartic effect. It's kind of like *The View* only with a lot of hair product and attractive people in the background.

I abbreviated the chain of events as best I could for her, covering the last disastrous dinner with her mother that started it all to our final call nearly two weeks ago. When I finished my story she said "You know what all that was about, don't you?" Having already read her mind, I merely raised my hand, which indicated to her my understanding.

I told Diedre about the apologetic text Shari sent me following our final conversation. Diedre's animation amused me as she stated disgustedly "OH WHATEVER!"

Diedre agreed with my philosophy: if Shari couldn't appreciate a partner who would go to bat for the relationship to work through the issues, then to hell with her. It is clearly her loss.

Right?

Day Twenty-Five: Bubble Gum Artistry

If I ever met the singer Meatloaf, I would ask him where he draws the line, since he says he would do "Anything For Love".

As I walked my dogs this morning, I observed something which made me pause. On the corner of the sidewalk, apparently where children gather for the school bus, was one sidewalk square unintentionally decorated with various colored spots of bubble gum on the concrete. I'm not sure, but I think it may have artistic value and I think Andy Warhol would side with me. I laugh that I've not only noticed this display, but that I was giving it an adequate amount of consideration. I admit it: it intrigued me. Graffiti intrigues me immensely too, but things like these are commonly thought of as remnants of human actions not worth examining. I disagree. I think many things are worth examining more closely, or at least deserving of a second look. After all, life *is* in the details.

Shari has a great appreciation for art: what would she think of this display? Would she respect my opinion on the matter? I'm slightly embarrassed to admit that I don't know the answer to either of those questions …

When driving in the car later in the afternoon, I pulled out my CD case which contained three CDs that Shari had made for me. The first one she gave to me upon our first meeting and the second and third ones were mailed to me at different points in our relationship. It reminded me of a *Friends* episode when Monica and Ross were discussing different levels of seriousness in a new relationship and referenced the act of giving the significant other "a mix tape." That made me laugh, because in essence, that is what I have!

A little nostalgia was stirred up listening to those songs, and thankfully it wasn't too painful. I started feeling a tad more sentimental as I listened to my Sia CD, though. I had purchased this CD right at the time Shari and I had first started dating, and soon after, the slow song "Moon" had become "our song." We never could make out all of the lyrics entirely, and only later after reading the lyrics inside the CD cover, discovered a discrepancy in the song's sentiment: Sia sang of a couple that would "never be" while we thought she was saying that they were "meant to be." (How ironic and foreboding was that?) We kept the song as our own despite the ominous theme, and just chose to modify the lyrics to our liking as we slow danced in Shari's living room on many, many occasions. Oh, how I miss dancing with her ...

It appeared that Amy and Rachel were having "mamma drama" again. Rachel's mother had resurrected her homophobic crusade against her daughter, much to Rachel and Amy's dismay. Rachel has come up with (in her mind) a temporary solution to at least fend off some of the oncoming attacks. When Amy comes to visit over the weekend, she should *hide her car in Rachel's garage.* This way when Rachel's prying family members prowl through the neighborhood, they won't become alarmed by Amy's apparent presence. I thought this was one of the WORST suggestions I had ever heard, and have begged Amy not to go along with it. Amy had confided in me that the entire situation was starting to make her uncomfortable, and understandably so!

I drew a parallel for Amy about something similar that occurred in my own relationship. If I would ever call Shari and she happened to be in the car with her mother, her mother would instantaneously start becoming as obnoxious as humanly possible in the background, guaranteed. The two of them could have been sitting in absolute silence until I called, and then, spontaneously, Shari's mother would break out into song, or just start talking incessantly. Although Shari (supposedly) found this as annoying as I did, her solution, was simply to not speak to me on the phone when she was in her mother's presence. I went along with this solution for awhile, until the day Shari "snuck a call" to me while on a road trip, when her mother exited the car to use the restroom. I thought to myself, "this is insane" and told Shari as much; I do believe she did finally (albeit reluctantly) address that issue with her mother. My point was that similarly Rachel's mother was forcing the two of them to modify *their* behavior, which wasn't right. Amy agreed and said she would remain steadfast in her decision to not hide her car, even if it screwed up their weekend plans. I surely hoped so.

Having felt confident that my anger towards Shari due to the tumultuousness of our fallout two weeks ago had adequately passed, I decided to attempt to call her. I did want the opportunity to apologize for my explosiveness when we parted (and admittedly I also wanted to know when my personal effects were going to be returned.) There was no answer when I called so my call was routed to voicemail; I opted to hang up. She would see that I attempted to call, and maybe call me back. If not, I would just send her a brief, polite email. It was getting somewhat late, and I was wondering why she didn't answer.

Was I being avoided?

Why would she avoid me, when I was the one upset with her?

Maybe she was in the shower?

Maybe she left her phone downstairs?

I had a fleeting thought that she may have been out, and could have been (though not likely) on a date, but that really didn't bother me. Why do I care? Because I don't want to think I am being avoided, that's why! Not only would that be adding insult to injury, but that would be just plain rude!

I proceeded to send my brief yet polite email before bed. We will see what tomorrow brings.

Day Twenty-Six: In Good Company

Rob Thomas of Matchbox 20 is part singer and part modern day philosopher, for he was right: our clarity truly does define us in the end ...

I checked my email first thing in the morning and found no response. This was peculiar. Logic told me that even if Shari didn't see my missed call until the morning that would have signaled to her that she probably had an email waiting for her. Oh well, maybe she'll check this afternoon.

A brief phone conversation with Tara confirmed my worst fear: "Oh, she is *totally* avoiding you. That's obvious." What a pleasant way to start the day!

Amy and Rachel are still having a stalemate. They are failing to reach a resolution, and it looks like Amy may be staying home today and going out to see Rachel tomorrow. I'm surprised by this, but think things will change at the last minute as they sometimes do.

Most of my morning and early afternoon was spent running work errands, so I did not get back in front of my computer until mid-day. I did find an email waiting for me from Shari. She was very formal yet polite and said she figured I was calling about my belongings. She just sent them out today and I should have my effects within a few days. (Amy said it was a good thing I did email her, or my stuff would be sitting there until Christmas. I tend to agree.) The most upsetting part of her email was when she shared with me that Boomer came down with kennel cough from being boarded at the vet! I replied to her email with a simple "thank you" to acknowledge her response, and left it at that. The whole exchange was somewhat sad to me, because you never would have known from those two emails that this was at one time a couple that talked about being "soulmates."

I'm not sure what triggered this memory, but later in the afternoon, I remembered something of significance regarding my past relationship, out of the blue. After about three months of dating, Shari and I embarked on a rather serious discussion regarding our future together. I asked her what her fears were, in terms of our relationship. Her answer to my question really resonated with me; she said "I'm afraid I don't have the necessary skills required to make a long-term relationship work." Retrospectively, I really (really) wish I had paid closer attention to that admission.

Fergie has a song out called "Big Girls Don't Cry" which reminds me of this scenario. If you haven't heard it, Fergie goes on to basically apologize to the sorry sap that has fallen in love with her because she has suddenly realized that she's got some personal issues to resolve before she can actually become involved in a relationship. Are you kidding me?? You mean you *really* didn't have a clue that you had these tendencies before you screwed with this poor individual's head? Or worse yet, you *knew* you had these issues, got involved with someone, and then *after* the relationship commenced, *then* you decide to divulge this little detail?? I think there should be some kind of screening process to keep these people out of the dating pool, or maybe some kind of registry for them to join like sex offenders. They would be known as "relationship offenders" and all have a big, fat disclaimer on their profiles warning the general public that despite their greatest *intentions*, these individuals have a historic tendency to devastate their partners with their spontaneous epiphanies. Enough of this "Oops, I did it again" crap!

Later on, I touched base with Amy to find out if her plans had changed at all, because I was certain that she was on her way to see

Rachel. Much to my surprise, they had agreed not to see each other today, and Amy would drive down to see Rachel tomorrow. (Well, I suppose that was one way to alleviate the hiding-the-car-in-the-garage dilemma.) I asked Amy if she had wanted to get together and "do something", which was my abbreviated way of suggesting we rent a movie. I recommended she come over to my family's house (admittedly out of sheer laziness because I didn't want to drive) and we would go to the video rental place together; she agreed, so I would be seeing Amy tonight, which was a rare treat.

When Amy arrived it was early evening, and I was anxious to see her because she was sporting a new hair cut. It turned out the hair cut was really cute! It was significantly shorter than what it was, but change is good, and sometimes we all need an immediate, significant change.

We drove down to the video store together and perused all of the new releases. While we were searching for our entertainment for the evening I asked her, "Do you remember when I told you I asked Shari way back when, what her relationship fear was?"

After a few seconds of thought Amy responded, "Yeah, didn't she say that she didn't have certain *skills?*"

I confirmed her answer and followed it up by saying, "Take a lesson from this: if someone tells you they don't have the "skills" to make a relationship work (and don't follow it up with 'but I'm working on that' or 'I'd like to see that change') LISTEN TO THEM, because chances are, they are telling you the truth!"

By the end of the evening, we realized that we had ended up making a poor movie selection, but I think the good company more than made up for the lackluster cinematography.

Day Twenty-Seven: Beloved Brunch

I'm ready to break out into the anthem
"We Are Family" by Sister Sledge!

It was another Sunday morning and today I was meeting Tara, Amy and Karen for brunch. The plan was to pick up Tara at her apartment and meet Karen and Amy downtown at the restaurant. I had already watched Joel Osteen, got ready and was out the door shortly thereafter. I wondered to myself if Shari still watches Joel on Sunday ...

I arrived at Tara's place somewhat late because this was my first time going to her new apartment; Tara is directionally challenged and was of virtually no assistance in this endeavor. The time I would have spent visiting and having tea with the woman has now been spent acquainting myself with Tara's entire neighborhood. By the time I arrived, I was slightly irritable, and Tara took that as her cue to be as fully cooperative as possible, and got into my car quickly so that we would still get to brunch on time.

Karen had suggested we meet at Magnolia Café which was located near an area of the city known as Uptown. We were able to park without too much difficulty. Amy was meeting us there. Karen in the meanwhile had sent me a text saying that she was with Amy, they had a table already, and were waiting inside.

When we walked in, I immediately spotted Karen and Amy sitting in a booth; Karen was waving enthusiastically when we walked in. The restaurant had a rather eclectic style and the warm colors made it feel most inviting. Reaching the table, we all exchanged customary hugs and chose our preferred seating. Karen looked great. She was sporting a tan from having been in California, and she had some caramel highlights in her naturally chestnut colored hair. Between her wardrobe and accessories Karen always looked well put together. Amy was looking her usual neat yet casual self. I, on the other hand, felt as though I was having a horrendous hair day, not to mention Tara and Karen were both teasing me about my sweater being zipped up too high, which automatically made me a "prude". I was tempted to tell Tara that the 80's called and said they wanted their hair back, but I bit my tongue (only because I had teased her about her big hair earlier in the day.)

Conversation quickly turned to the latest events between Karen and Angel. Last I had heard, Karen had basically told Angel to take a proverbial hike. Now we came to learn that the two have not only been talking, but Angel is supposedly still planning on coming to live with Karen! I was disgusted and would have been on the verge of losing my appetite, had the cinnamon apple stuffed French toast not sounded so heavenly. I was trying so hard not to sound like a bitter divorcee, or particularly cynical, but I was not an advocate of this relationship between Karen and Angel, and proceeded to voice that fact (yet again.) Tara and Amy were quickly brought up to speed on the situation between Karen and Angel and were privy to all of my concerns for Karen's sake. Tara sympathized with Karen, and in defense of our naïve friend, began to formulate a theory about the objectivity of those caught up in romance. Tara was trying to convince me that Karen could not be held responsible for her actions because she was under the influence of Love's spell. What is this, a twisted episode of *Boston Legal*? Are we attempting to claim "innocent by reason of insanity"? What happened to good old-fashioned common sense? Amy agreed that Karen should be exercising better judgment, but then defaulted to "if she's happy…"

I wasn't paying complete attention to their arguments though as I was eyeing the raspberry which was seducing me from the bottom of Karen's glass of champagne.

A mini-argument then commenced after Karen and Tara decided to challenge me with a hypothetical scenario (to which Amy remained neutral.) They asked me if Shari moved to Chicago, said she wanted to work things out, and she had already started therapy, would I take her back? I said no. They didn't believe me. I said no again, based on the fact that I have had too much time to reflect on a variety of issues in this particular relationship. They still did not believe me. It was aggravating me because I knew they were not listening to what I was saying, but rather, projecting their own feelings about their relationships onto mine, and assuming I feel (or would feel) the same way...or maybe they know me better than I know myself at this point. (What was that Tara was saying about the objectivity of those in love?)

Although our table was engrossed in conversation, we couldn't help but notice that across the room at another booth, three apparent lesbians were talking about us, or at least about one of us. I gathered from their glances and giggling that they were referencing Karen. I say *apparent* lesbians because they were clearly of a more stereotypically masculine caliber; to the untrained eye, our table could have passed for a group of straight women while this clearly would not have been the case with our imitation boy band at the other table. They were dressed rather fashionably, I had to give them that, though. One butch in particular had on designer jeans, and a stylish, black leather jacket with a t-shirt on underneath (which I would have bet read, "Nice legs...What time do they open?") We touched on the topic of the obnoxiousness of our counterparts nearby, just as our food was being served, and conversation soon shifted to who had the yummiest entree.

When it came time to leave, as fate would have it, we found ourselves leaving at nearly the same time as the undesirable trio. We briefly debated deliberately waiting for the offensive women to vacate the restaurant before making our own exit. The more I thought about it though, a part of me was becoming angry that we had to inconvenience ourselves due to others' ignorance. We collectively decided to make our way to the front. We had settled the bill, put on our coats and were preparing to leave the restaurant, when one of our boy band members addressed Karen at the door, at the goading of her companions.

"So what's the deal? Are you a man or a woman?" The blatant crudeness of her question stunned all of us …or almost all of us.

Without batting an eyelash Karen coolly responded, "That's funny because I was just about to ask you the same thing."

Tara laughed out loud, Amy smiled in approval, and I proudly held the door open for my friend, declaring "Ladies first."

Day Twenty-Eight: Final Day

After all is said and done, we have both ended up "Bent" ...

I realize that today is my final day of my journaling, and I believe I will actually miss it. I am very, very sorry to have contributed to the circumstances which led to this project in the first place, but it has been a bit of a learning experience. I debate whether or not I should send a copy of this to Shari ...

(then of course the nasty side of me says, "Hell, she can *buy* her own copy!")

I was out most of the day on sales calls today, and when I returned, there was an email waiting for me from Karen. I never expected the email to express the sentiment it did: she had asked me out on an "official" date. She had chosen to do this via email, and left me explicit instructions that if I was not interested, to not respond, and we could pretend none of this ever happened. Does she really think I operate this way? I wonder who would operate this way?

I had multiple reactions to this occurrence, and several justifications as to why this should not and would not take place. First and foremost, we are friends and I did not want to jeopardize this relationship. Second, my own romantic wounds are so fresh that they are still scabbing over, so I can't possibly imagine dating *anyone* for quite some time. I addressed this issue this in typical, head-on style, and I called Karen.

Karen was apparently quite embarrassed by the situation, and repeatedly stated that she wished I had followed the instructions given to me in the email. I claimed that it was better to actually speak about this, although, truth be told, it was not a conversation that I was particularly looking forward to either!

I proceeded to methodically give her my reasons for why we could not go out on a date, beginning with the protection of the current relationship we shared and the consideration which should be given to my own healing heart. She did not agree with my arguments, but she did agree to respect my decision.

I was happy and relieved.

Much later after our phone call, I had found myself wondering how Karen could have even asked me out when she claimed that she was expecting Angel to "come home" within the month.

Sometimes what we *tend to believe* and what we instinctually *know* end up being two completely different things.

But ignorance is still bliss.

Epilogue: Final Dream Analysis

*I promise: not a single "I Told You So" if we
can end this craziness right now!*

On the 29th day of my breakup, I had a dream right before waking up that I was in New York with Shari. I know it was New York because we were in a building…a hotel…that had a clear view of the city skyline. I was very sorry that I did not write this as soon as I awoke because some of the details of the dream have since faded. Shari did play an extensive role in this dream, instead of the traditional cameo appearance she provided in the past. I do remember that we were supposed to meet a couple of Shari's old college friends. In my dream, we were meeting two very tall men who spoke German. I remember being a little put off by the difficulty in communicating with them and the fact that they were so tall and looming, literally looking down on me. The elevator in the hotel would slowly spin as it ascended or descended, so instead of just letting you off on a particular floor, it would deposit you on a certain angle leading you to a certain room. (This made it even more difficult to reach your intended destination right away!) I remembered feeling stressed riding the elevator because I was clearly on a mission, and I remembered feeling a little frustrated and uncomfortable once I had finally reached Shari and her friends.

On the thirtieth day after my breakup I did in fact receive my personal effects in the mail, as Shari had predicted. She sent me back more items than I requested, but what struck me acutely and made me very sad, was that there was no note in the box. It was just a box full of miscellaneous items. When I sent Shari her belongings back, I did include a note that simply said, "You were *my* 'Big Love'."

Nearly one month had gone by since the last time we had spoken on the phone, when I noticed that I had left one more important item at her house: a pair of shoes. I ended up sending her an email which resulted in a back-and-forth exchange about the location of my beloved footwear. By the third day of this, her cold tone was wearing on me during the email communication, so I decided to call her.

I asked her immediately if she was upset with me because of the curt tone of her emails. She confessed that it was more of a defense mechanism than anything, and apologized. She missed me, and admitted that her behavior was quite reactionary. We chatted for awhile and overall had a pleasant conversation. It was so pleasant as a matter of fact that we spoke the next day, the day after, and the next day after that ...

I ended up telling her about the "Love Is" I had cut out of the newspaper and wanted to send her, and she told me about a satirical "Love Is" that she had seen on a t-shirt that said "Love is…having matching tattoos" which naturally made her think of us, due to our running joke about the topic.

I came to the realization during our conversation that I did leave yet another item at her house: a set of lingerie she had bought me for Christmas. She surely must have seen the articles since I left. Was she keeping it as an intimate momento or was it going to be used as some kind of Cinderella's slipper for whatever bimbo she hooked up with in the future? I broached the topic in this way:

"Did you run across any other items of mine when you were gathering my things to send?"

"No. That was everything."

"Are you sure?" I ask.

"Yes, I'm sure. I searched thoroughly."

I paused a moment and then declared, "You still have the lingerie from Christmas, you know."

"Yes, I know" she responded without hesitation.

Ok, she just outright lied to me, and quite unapologetically I might add!

"You just said you didn't have anything else!"

"Well, I wasn't going to mention it if you weren't! I saw it and thought, 'I'll be damned if I'm going to send her the lingerie I bought for her to wear for some other bitch!'"

I reminded her, "You know, much like the steak dinner, Love, it appears as though you really do have trouble giving *unconditionally*."

My point was taken and she offered to send the lingerie if I really wanted it. I declined, not wanting to cause her any more mental anguish than what I was already responsible for.

As our conversation progressed I was moved to ask her if she felt that the demise of our relationship might affect her perspective on future relationships with other women; I revealed that as a result of our breakup I thought that I might have trouble believing my lovers in the future (or at the very least believing that they really knew what they wanted.) She confessed that our breakup left her feeling "more cynical than ever" regarding relationships. (Well, as long as a good time was had by all!)

By the fourth day of exchanging emails, texts and phone calls, things were feeling eerily familiar, as though time had stood still, and nothing had really changed. Did we break up? I brought this to her attention, and she agreed. I was starting to feel mildly uncomfortable with going through the motions of our routine when we had been a couple, when we were still clearly no longer a couple; it was confusing. Of course over these past four days we had discussed our breakup, and both entertained the thought of reconciliation, but with nothing resulting except more confusion.

I shared with Shari a rather depressing and profound thought that had occurred to me during this period of resurrected communication: some people spend their entire lives searching for someone to love, and in our case we had been deliberately spending time trying to erase the memories of our relationship, seemingly against our wills. To me, the irony was almost laughable. Shari had even admitted to me that breaking up wasn't what she necessarily *wanted* to do, but rather something that she "*had* to do" ...

That evening, as we spoke on the phone, I went out on a limb and asked her to come to Chicago for the weekend. I really wanted to see her, and I wanted to know if the feelings were mutual. She did show some interest but offered a few reasons as to why the upcoming weekend wasn't "convenient." My revived disappointment prompted me to make a suggestion: if we were going to keep speaking to one another in the immediate future, and attempt to be in one another's lives, then we had to establish some boundaries (at the very least, for *my* sanity's sake.) I felt as though over the past four days I had been receiving some mixed messages, which she admitted to sending. I suggested that we agree after this evening to not indulge in any intimate conversation and not to reference nostalgic particulars about our former relationship in order for our aspiring friendship to flourish. She reluctantly agreed and I was happy and secure in my belief that starting tomorrow we could begin working on our new relationship as friends.

We ended the conversation warmly and admittedly I felt a small sense of relief knowing that Shari was back in my life sans the drama ... or so I thought.

The End

*I never thought in a million years, that we'd
end up just another "Picture to Burn"...*

I woke up this morning feeling good that Shari and I had finally reached a decision on how to best deal with our attempts to communicate, while still being respectful of our new set boundaries. This was our fifth consecutive day of speaking, and Shari had called me wanting my opinion on an idea she had: she wanted to know what I had thought about her coming out to Chicago in three weeks to see me, over Memorial Day weekend! I shook my head while on the phone and thought, "We were so close to pulling this friendship thing off!"

I questioned why this was occurring, to which she responded, "I really *do* want to see you." I had actually made peace with our decision from the night before, and now she had to do this?? The conversation did not end here but continued throughout the morning during bursts of intermittent phone calls back and forth, because we were both unable to commit ourselves to ten solid minutes of uninterrupted conversation.

By the early afternoon we were able to set aside a short amount of time to have a real discussion on the matter. I had said that as much as I did want to see her, after having given it adequate thought, if we were no closer to reaching a resolution to get back together, then there really wasn't a point to meeting; it would be too difficult for the both of us. I may be a masochist at times, but not that much of a masochist!

As our conversation continued, we predictably started delving into past topics such as therapy, her mother, and our relationship as a whole.

I stated in an exhausted tone, "Shari, we both know how hard it is to find a partner to even *consider* becoming serious with. That being said, I think that the most anyone can hope for is to find a partner who is open-minded, takes responsibility for their faults, and genuinely wants to compromise and seek resolution for the sake of the relationship."

(I have the proverbial stove in my sights.)

Her response came slowly; she could see my point, but in her opinion, "too many bridges have been burned and too much irreparable damage has occurred in the relationship."

I asked mildly sarcastically, "In whose relationship? Ours? Or the one between me and your mother?"

(The stove is beckoning me like a siren in the sea.)

She gradually admitted the damage had more to do with me and her mother, but went on to explain how that damage directly impacted our situation. She said that they were a kind of "package deal" and made the comparison to dating someone who has a child, if the other partner has an aversion to children. I said that was not necessarily a fair analogy (although secretly I found the comparison amusing.)

"I think you have distinct personality issues" Shari states.

I could not decipher whether the "you" in that sentence was directed towards me solely, or if she was implying that her mother and I had a special dynamic so I asked her to clarify.

(My hand is now hovering over the stove.)

"More than one person has told me that you're a bitch...and I just can't be with that."

(AND WE HAVE CONTACT! I have instantaneous third degree burns!)

Several seconds of silence ensued, which prompted her to ask me if I was thinking. I was indeed thinking ... several retaliatory things at that moment, actually, but was restraining myself from saying them out loud.

Initially, I thought, "Wow … I can't believe I was just insulted … *again.*" I needed a few moments to admire my freshly-acquired emotional blisters. When I was sure I was in control of myself, I calmly stated, "Perhaps it is better if we resume our non-speaking regimen, and maybe down the road we can revisit the idea." She replied with her standard lackluster "okay", and we ended the conversation. I knew at that moment it would be a very long time before we would speak again, if ever.

It was a Saturday night and I was sitting in the backyard accompanied by my two dogs, feeling rather mellow and particularly introspective. My parents were going out to dinner and they attempted to coax me into going with them, sensing that I may have been somewhat blue. I assured them that I was fine, thanked them for their offer and concern and encouraged them to go have a nice evening. After they had left, I resumed my state of self-analysis. A few days had passed since my last phone conversation with Shari, and I was feeling increasingly out of sorts replaying our final exchange. I desperately needed to put an end to all of this melodrama once and for all.

I went to the garage and not too effortlessly dug out an old, small barbeque grill I still had from years past and carried it to the backyard patio. It was far from a decorative firebowl, but it would serve the purpose. I then went inside the house and gathered all of the personal relics of my relationship with Shari which I had saved (naturally) in a shoebox. Returning back outside on the patio, matches in hand, I proceeded to place all of the intimate effects into the grill. By using a Valentine's Day card as the fiery catalyst, I soon had the entire grill's contents ablaze …

I wouldn't have thought it was possible, but my heart felt like it was breaking all over again …

Maybe my idea of catharsis was a little "over the top", but admittedly, my need for closure took precedent over anything else. Silly as it may be, deep in the recesses of my imagination (the part that governs gothic romance) a small secreted part of me hoped that the destruction of those effects would break what felt like a relentless spell on my heart. I must confess that I had never experienced such a sense of loss. I have experienced heartbreak before, but this felt vastly different. It's hard to explain, but on a few rare occasions in the midst of feeling relatively at ease about our breakup, I could spontaneously be hit with such an overwhelming emptiness that it brought with it a feeling of anxiety, like that of a mild panic attack. I'm grateful that those extreme episodes were far and few in between.

Not a single day had gone by that I hadn't thought about Shari, and I was sure that would continue for quite some time. I sincerely loved her with all of my heart; I will always wish things could have gone differently, but I do believe that everything happens for a reason, and I am positive that in the future I will be a better friend and a better girlfriend for having had this experience.

The evening was winding down and I began to entertain myself with the daydream of Cher joining me in the backyard for that cup of tea and the two of us admiring the sparsely starlit sky together as we settled into a meditative, quiet comfort. Inevitably, she would break the silence and ask me the impending question, "*Do you* believe in life after love?"

I would lean back in my chair, and after a moment smile thoughtfully and reply, "Absolutely."

Christine Hutman, creator of the Chicago based website, PetServicesReview.com, lives in New Jersey with her wife, Shannon, their two dogs, Pepper and Nikita, their cat, Flame, and will soon be welcoming two turkeys (yes, turkeys) to the family. Christine is currently working on her second book.

Christine can be reached via email through the book's website, www.CrazyLesbianBreakup.com.

www.ingramcontent.com/pod-product-compliance
Lightning Source LLC
Chambersburg PA
CBHW061304280526
45784CB00002B/892